OFFA'S DYKE
PATH SOUTH

NATIONAL TRAIL GUIDES

OFFA'S DYKE PATH SOUTH

Chepstow to Knighton

Ernie and Kathie Kay and Mark Richards

Photographs by Archie Miles

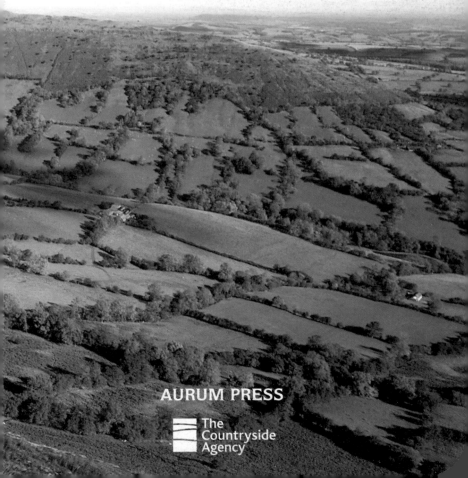

AURUM PRESS

The
Countryside
Agency

ACKNOWLEDGEMENTS

Special thanks are due to Jim Saunders, the Offa's Dyke Development Officer (for the Countryside Council for Wales and Powys County Council) and Dave McGlade, his field assistant, for advice and checking changes. Also to Peter Mayes for his assistance with the circular walks.

Ernie Kay, and his late wife Kathy, have been associated with the Welsh border for the past 35 years. They helped plan Offa's Dyke Path and are founder members and officers of the Offa's Dyke Association; they now live right on the Offa's Dyke Path. Mark Richards is well known as an illustrator and author of guide books.

This revised edition first published 2000 by Aurum Press Ltd in association with the Countryside Agency
Text copyright © 1989, 1994, 2000 by Aurum Press Ltd and the Countryside Agency
Maps Crown copyright © 1989, 1994, 2000 by the Ordnance Survey
Photographs copyright © 1989, 1994 by the Countryside Agency

Ordnance Survey and Pathfinder are registered trade marks and the OS Symbol, Explorer and Outdoor Leisure are trade marks of Ordnance Survey, the National Mapping Agency of Great Britain.

A catalogue record for this book is available from the British Library

ISBN 185410 671 6

1 3 5 4 2
2000 2002 2003 2004

Book design by Robert Updegraff

Cover photograph: Offa's Dyke looking south from the Lugg Valley
Title page photograph: The Cat's Back Ridge from Hatterall Ridge

Typeset by Wyvern Typesetting Ltd, Bristol
Printed and bound in Italy by Printer Trento Srl

CONTENTS

Circular walks appear on pages 31, 36, 43, 45, 60, 72, 75, 80, 85, 89, 102, 104, 118 and 120.

How to use this guide

The 177-mile (285-kilometre) Offa's Dyke Path is covered by two national trail guides. This book features the southern section of the Path, from Chepstow to Knighton (80 miles/129 kilometres including sections through towns). A companion guide features the Path from Knighton to Prestatyn.

The guide is in three parts:

• The introduction, with an historical background to the area and advice for walkers.

• The Path itself, split into five chapters, with maps opposite the description for each route section. This part of the guide also includes information on places of interest as well as a number of short walks which can be taken around each part of the Path. Key sites are numbered both in the text and on the maps to make it easier to follow the route description.

• The last part includes useful information such as local transport, accommodation and organisations involved with the Path.

The maps have been prepared by Ordnance Survey® for this trail guide using 1:25000 Pathfinder®, Explorer™ or Outdoor Leisure™ maps as a base. The line of Offa's Dyke Path is shown in yellow, with the status of each section of the Path—footpath or bridleway, for example—shown in green underneath (see key on inside front cover). These rights of way markings also indicate the precise alignment of the Path, which walkers should follow. In some cases, the yellow line may show a route which is different from that shown on older maps; walkers are recommended to follow the yellow route in this guide, which will be the route that is waymarked with the distinctive acorn symbol ♣ used for all national trails. Some sections of the Path may be shown following a line of black dots, since the base map available at the time of producing this edition does not have up-to-date details of the public rights of way over which Offa's Dyke Path goes. Any parts of the Path that may be difficult to follow on the ground are clearly highlighted in the route description, and important points to watch for are marked with letters in each chapter, both in the text and on the maps. *Some maps start on a right-hand page and continue on the left-hand page— black arrows (➡) at the edge of the maps indicate the start point.* Should there be a need to divert the Path from the route shown in this guide, for maintenance work or because the route has had to be changed, walkers are advised to follow any waymarks or signs along the Path.

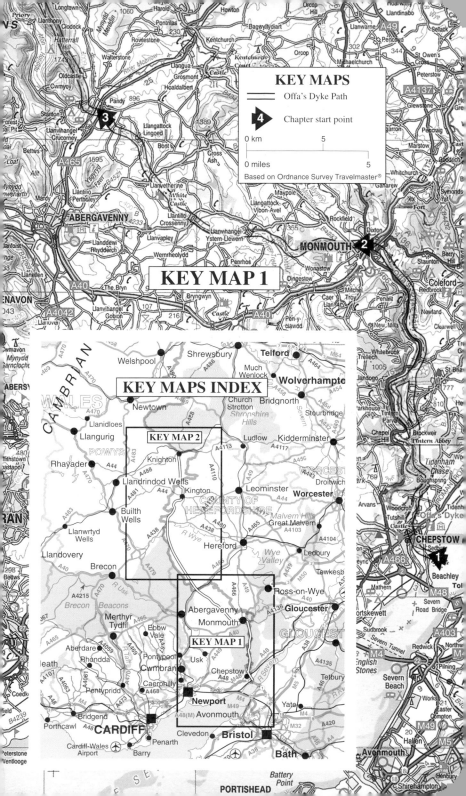

KEY MAPS

— Offa's Dyke Path

▶ **4** Chapter start point

0 km   5

0 miles   5

Based on Ordnance Survey Travelmaster®

KEY MAP 1

KEY MAPS INDEX

KEY MAP 2

KEY MAP 1

KEY MAP 2

Distance checklist

This list will assist you in calculating the distances between places on the southern half of the Path where you may be planning to stay overnight, or in checking your progress along the way.

location	approx. distance from previous location	
	miles	km
Sedbury Cliffs	0	0
Former A48 (for Chepstow)	1.8	2.9
Bigsweir (for St Briavels)	8.6*	13.8
Redbrook	3.5	5.6
Monmouth	3.6	5.8
Llantilio Crossenny	9.2	14.8
White Castle	2.1	3.4
Pandy	5.5	8.9
Hatterrall (Longtown to Llanthony path)	4.5	7.2
Pen-y-Beacon (Hay Bluff) (off official route)	8.6	13.8
Hay-on-Wye	4.4	7.0
Newchurch	6.5	10.5
Gladestry	3.7	6.0
Kington	4.5	7.2
Dolley Green	7.9	12.7
Knighton	5.6	9.0

*Using upper route from Brockweir to Bigsweir; 9.6 miles (15.4 km) using riverside route.

PREFACE

The Offa's Dyke Path traces, for much of its length, the ancient earthwork which gives it its name. Criss-crossing the modern borders of England and Wales this National Trail runs from Chepstow on the Severn Estuary to Prestatyn on the Irish Sea coast of North Wales. This book covers the southern section as far as Knighton: a companion volume, *Offa's Dyke Path North*, continues the journey to Prestatyn.

The variety of scenery on this stretch of the path is remarkable, from the wooded and dramatic Wye Valley it skirts the Black Mountains to Hay-on-Wye before following Hergest Ridge to Kington where it bears due north and tracks several stretches of the Dyke to Knighton. No fewer than ten circular walks described in this book make the path attractive to day visitors as well as to the seasoned long-distance walker.

National Trails are promoted and funded by the Countryside Agency and maintained by local authorities. Like other National Trails, the path is waymarked with the distinctive acorn symbol which signals that you are on the right route.

I hope that you will enjoy this book during many hours of walking on this delightful journey through the border lands of England and Wales.

Ewen Cameron
Chairman
The Countryside Agency

Foreword

by Lord Hunt of Llanfair Waterdine, KG

I treasure the memory of a hot summer's day in July 1971 when, at my home town of Knighton, I declared open the long distance route along the line of Offa's Dyke, at the invitation of the Countryside Commission [now the Countryside Agency]. For my wife and myself this marked a high point in our long association with the Welsh Border, which had begun nearly thirty years earlier. It was, indeed, almost (but not quite!) as memorable a moment as the welcome I received in the town and in our parish of Llanfair Waterdine after my return from Everest in 1953. The Dyke itself follows the high ground just above our old home and our present cottage in the parish, so the reader will, I hope, forgive me, as a past-President of the Offa's Dyke Association, for feeling especially sentimental, almost proprietorial, about the Dyke. I have sampled many other national trails; each has its special attractions, but the Offa's Dyke Path holds pride of place in my affections.

To celebrate the opening event, we set off that same day in 1971 on a four-day trek northwards towards the terminus of the Dyke Path at Prestatyn; the prevailing heatwave and the bracken flies detracted not at all from a journey which, for us, held some of the illusory magic of trail-blazing. As so often in a busy life, time was our enemy; it was only a year later that we were able to complete our acquaintance with the Dyke by walking southwards, from Spoad Farm in the valley of the Clun, to reach its end on the red cliffs overlooking the River Severn.

But more important than this personal connection is the link which the Dyke provides with the distant past in the story of our nation. Often, standing on Llanfair hill above our cottage, I have had a strong sense of a dim, unrecorded age, before invaders from across the North Sea forced our Celtic ancestors westwards into Wales. Long before King Offa caused the construction of his monumental earthwork, I seem to perceive, through

11

the mists of time, those tribal people in their upland dwellings who grew corn on the high ground and hunted deer and wild boar in the densely forested Teme Valley down below. I have, too, a sense of that still-distant but recorded past; of the wars and skirmishes between Romans and Celts, Normans and Welshmen, which were fought around the hill forts and castles which provide one of the main attractions of this national trail. Indeed, I believe that it is not mere fantasy to suggest that, while walking along Offa's Dyke, the past is still with us in the present.

However this may be, I hope that readers of this guidebook will share my own delight in the scenery it affords and the ancient history which it conjures up.

John Hunt

PART ONE

INTRODUCTION

'Not the oldest, nor the longest, but the best.' So said Lord Sandford about the Offa's Dyke Path at an Annual General Meeting of the Offa's Dyke Association, of which he was then President. This Path is based not on a geographical feature, but on a man-made historic one, and to this it owes the variety of its scenery. It may not have the high lonely moorland of the Pennine Way, nor the sparkling sea views of the coastal paths, but it is unique in the different kinds of countryside through which it passes and the strange stories of the past told by the historic features seen on the way.

Historical background: a frontier zone

The Welsh Border, though it has not always been a frontier in the modern sense, lies along the division between the Welsh uplands to the west and the lower ground of the English Midlands to the east. There is no single edge, but a variety of hills, so the exact position of this boundary has varied from age to age.

Early peoples would not have formed the concept of a boundary line; nevertheless, this area often acted as a division between peoples who felt a need to protect themselves from neighbours of different origin. Thus some of the most striking early signs of occupation on the hilltops are the hill forts, which are very numerous throughout the Border and include some of the largest and most complex fortifications found anywhere in the world. They are usually thought to date from the Iron Age, just before the Roman invasion of Britain, but recent investigations show that some originated in the Bronze Age, as long ago as 1200 BC, with some ramparts dating back to 800 BC, and occupation sometimes lasting for more than 1,000 years. The forts were certainly still in use for native defence against the Romans: somewhere in these Border hills Caractacus must have made his last stand before being taken as a captive to Rome, but we cannot be sure exactly where.

The Romans themselves also left their mark on the area, with remains of forts, roads and other structures, but they pushed on westwards without establishing any boundary feature as they had at Hadrian's Wall. The first marked line must be the feature that most concerns us on this Path, Offa's Dyke itself – believed to date from the late 8th century – but of this more later.

The Border remained an area of conflict. William the Conqueror must have recognised the threat, for he made grants of land to powerful 'Marcher' barons, who built defensive castles in the area known as the Welsh 'Marches'. The word 'Marches' comes from the same origin as 'Mark', possibly referring to Offa's Dyke itself. It does not refer to walking, or the season of the year and certainly not to damp marshland! Norman lords, and their successors until the late 15th century, the 'Lords Marchers' (who are not a cricket team raising money for charity), were granted lands in the Welsh Border area. Many claimed special rights, not subject to the normal restraints of English law, over a wide, imprecise area which they held and ruled by right of conquest. Their castles range from the numerous earth mounds of the 'motte and bailey' type to great stone buildings, still forbidding after seven or eight centuries of neglect and decay, such as Chepstow and Rhuddlan. The Welsh fought back and there was frequent Border conflict until the defeat of Owain Glyndwr in 1410. They built castles too; Dinas Bran, above Llangollen, is the most impressive you will see.

With the castles came other features that still survive. The Marcher strongholds were often accompanied by the establishment of a 'borough', usually a planned town. Some decayed, some never developed, but many tiny villages still retain a complicated grid layout. For the common people, the nearest refuge in case of alarm was usually the church, often built with a strong defensive 'Border' tower. Many of these have survived, while the rest of the medieval fabric has decayed or been replaced by something more fashionable.

In later centuries, the hills which had divided peoples were important for minerals and water power, and many parts of the Border became important centres of early industry. Some of these still survive, particularly east of the Clwydian Hills; elsewhere the remains of mills, tramways and minepits survive in areas from which the bustle of industry has long departed.

From the times of peace many graceful domestic buildings also remain, ranging from stately mansions to the timber-framed farmhouses and cottages for which the Border is noted.

Tintern Abbey seen through the mist from Offa's Dyke at Shorn Cliff.

Offa's Dyke – when, where, why and how?

For over half its length the Path keeps company with the Dyke that gives it its name. Sometimes it is a great bank up to 25 feet (7.6 metres) high, with a deep ditch to the west; at other times it is no more than a hedgebank or a ridge across a ploughed field, identifiable only because it is 'in the right place'. In some parts where you might expect to find it, for instance in the quite low-lying areas north of Monmouth, the Dyke seems not to be there at all. This unpredictability has led to much scholarly speculation and dispute about the Dyke.

When was it built? Strangely, no contemporary records relating to its construction or early use have been found. The first positive reference comes about 100 years after the attributed date of construction, when Asser, Bishop of Sherborne but previously from Wales, tells us positively that King Offa ordered a great Dyke to be built between Wales and Mercia, stretching from sea to sea. The lack of contemporary mention has caused some to doubt whether Offa did indeed build the Dyke, or whether it may have existed earlier. However, there seems little reason to doubt the later records, tradition and the evidence of place names on the line. After the Romans, Offa was probably the first ruler to have the power and organisation to carry out work on this scale, and the appearance and alignment of the whole earthwork suggest that it must have been conceived as a whole.

It may then seem strange that there should be any doubt about *where* the Dyke runs. The most problematical area is in the north, where recent excavation has thrown doubt on whether any of the fragmentary remains north of Treuddyn, identified by Sir Cyril Fox in his survey of the earthwork in the 1920s and 1930s, are in fact part of the Dyke. As a result, Dr David Hill of Manchester University, who has directed the work in this area, has concluded that the other Dyke further to the east, known as Wat's Dyke, might well be the northern section of Offa's. In the southern parts, where Fox often attributed the absence of dyke to impenetrable forest, Frank Noble's detailed studies identified traces in several areas where it had been thought missing, as well as explaining certain of the gaps. David Hill now considers that the stretch of Dyke above the Wye Valley may date from a different period and thus not be part of the same earthwork!

Why was the Dyke built? Fox's view was that it was a

boundary marker – quite an awe-inspiring one! – rather than an actual defensive work. However, both Hill and Noble, in their detailed studies, eventually concluded that the form and siting of the Dyke pointed to defence, possibly with added fortifications, such as a stockade, and with the intention of permanent manning. Suggestions that the Dyke might have been an ancient trackway are quite at odds with its profile and the steep gradients it traverses: fine for walkers, and for defence, but hardly a convenient route!

As to *how* it was constructed, the controversial questions are whether the entire Dyke was built by a single expert construction team, or whether local gangs of workers were responsible for their individual stretches. The second theory would explain some of the odd anomalies, such as the strange right-angled bends at Hergan where two teams may have failed to meet, or the abrupt change from high dyke to low bank on the hill just south of Knighton, but there is no certain evidence.

The landscape along the Path

Because Offa's Dyke and its Path do not follow a single natural feature, they pass through a succession of landscape forms of great variety. These are derived from the underlying rocks and support an equal variety of types of natural vegetation and farming activity.

In the far south the Path is high on the eastern edge of the spectacular limestone cliffs of the lower Wye Valley which form the western edge of the Forest of Dean plateau, an area rich in coal and other minerals and one of the earliest industrial areas. Rocks of the older Devonian age underlie most of the route from Monmouth to Hay but produce two very different land forms; the rolling farmlands of the Monnow and Trothy Valleys and then the spectacular hills of the Black Mountains, supporting only a few sheep and ponies.

The northbound walker follows the north–south 'grain' of the landscape up to Hay, while north of the upper Wye Valley for a long way the lie of the land is east–west over a terrain formed from the underlying Silurian rocks. Landforms again vary from rounded moorlands such as Hergest Ridge and grassy hills such as Hawthorn, Llanfair and Long Mountain, supporting mainly sheep and, increasingly, conifers, to the fertile river valleys of the Arrow, Lugg, Teme, Caebitra and Camlad where cattle flourish. Many of the Silurian rocks are shales producing a building stone that crumbles with age. You will see many buildings constructed of this material falling into ruin. An example is the old primary school at Knighton, now the Offa's Dyke Centre; the Youth Hostel in the same building is currently (1994) closed pending structural repairs.

Below Long Mountain the Severn is crossed and its flat alluvial valley, good for cattle but liable to flooding, is followed north to Llanymynech. Seen to the east are the volcanic Breidden Hills.

Beyond Llanymynech the Path rises again on the west edge of hills of Carboniferous rocks which produce both the old industrial landscapes of west Shropshire and the spectacular limestone crags of the Eglwyseg above Llangollen and the Dee Valley.

A short stretch of peaty moorland, increasingly under conifers, is crossed south of Llandegla and the Path then climbs on to the barren north–south moors of the Clwydian Hills, another Silurian ridge. This is sandwiched between the alluvial Clwyd Vale to the west, with the volcanic summits of Snowdonia seen beyond, and the Flintshire–Wrexham industrial area, based on Carboniferous Limestone and Coal Measures, to the east. The Dyke itself, but not the Path, goes right through this industrial belt. In its final section the Path is on Carboniferous rocks in a mixed area of moors, pastures and woods until you reach high cliffs above the sands of the North Wales coast.

This description can give only a very simplified account of a complex geological pattern. The way this is reflected in the scenery is evident to the walker. The natural landscape determines the land use pattern, though the extent of new commercial forestry varies. In the long-established 'scenic' areas, such as the Black Mountains and Clwydian Hills, there has been a determined attempt to keep at least the hilltops free of trees.

These areas are the only ones on the route where real hill farming (usually sheep, though ponies are often grazed) is extensive. Elsewhere farms are being amalgamated, with some dereliction of buildings and removal of hedges, but less so than in many other parts of the country. Small fields for livestock still predominate, resulting in the plethora of stiles for which Offa's Dyke Path is 'famous'. It is still too early to tell what the long-term effects will be of current government policies to reduce the numbers of cattle and take land out of agricultural production.

Offa's Dyke Path on Hatterrall Hill, looking south towards Skirrid Fawr.

The origins and management of the Path

The idea of national trails, as they are called today, was set out in the National Parks and Access to the Countryside Act 1949, and Offa's Dyke was among the first to be suggested, but the whole idea took some time to get under way. The first trail, the Pennine Way, was not opened officially until 1965. Bodies such as the Ramblers' Association and local activists, including the newly founded Offa's Dyke Association, campaigned for the speedy opening of the other suggested paths. A certain amount of informal waymarking and clearance took place and this activity apparently impressed the Countryside Commission. Most of the outstanding negotiations were expedited, and the county councils, as agents of the Commission, were enjoined to erect stiles and waymarks. Eventually all this bore fruit at an opening ceremony in 1971, performed by Lord Hunt in the presence of the Chairman of the Countryside Commission, two government ministers and the largest crowd ever known to have assembled in the small Border town of Knighton.

Of course, more work remained to be done, and there is a continuing need for maintenance. Some 'permissive' stretches of Path have been made rights of way, Diversion Orders have been put into effect and many of the original stiles and way-marks have been replaced. Volunteers from the Offa's Dyke Association watch over conditions on every stretch of the route, report major problems and carry out minor works themselves. The Path crosses the Welsh–English border many times, two-thirds being in Wales and the remainder in England. The problems caused by the passing of the Countryside Commission's responsibilities in Wales to the new Countryside Council for Wales in 1991 have been resolved by the latter body coordinating management of the Path on behalf of both bodies. CCW now funds two full-time National Trail Officers, based in Knighton, who work closely with the Association and county highway authorities to maintain and promote the Path. All this care and attention means that Offa's Dyke is kept in excellent condition.

How to walk the Path

Waymarking. Each county highway authority chooses its own design of stiles and signs, so you will find considerable variation as you walk. Several types of marker are in use: wooden, and in some cases, metal, finger posts; concrete signs (sometimes irreverently described as 'tombstones' or even 'hydrants' because of their appearance); coloured arrows attached to, or painted on, fences and stiles; and acorns, the universal sign of a national trail, which are usually found on the stiles themselves. 'Usually' because, although all stiles were intended to be so identified, there have been occasional unofficial replacements by farmers, and also because the original metal symbols have proved irresistible to some unprincipled souvenir hunters.

Where the route is unclear, for instance at a junction of paths, you should find a sign to set you on your way, but, although a few walkers claim to have walked on waymarks alone, we do not recommend you to do this. If you also use the maps and description in this book, you should have no difficulty in finding the way.

Do not think, because the Path seldom rises to mountainous heights, that you are in for an easy stroll. In many parts, of which the 'Switchback' stretch north of Knighton is most notorious, the repeated rises and falls on the route mean that in the course of an average day's walk you climb the equivalent of a very considerable mountain. Do not discount the stiles, either: during the fieldwork for this book we counted nearly 700.

The surface, too, is very variable, and in some places makes walking difficult, such as on the boggy tops of the Black Mountains and the moors south of Llandegla, on steep slopes in many parts which become slippery in wet weather and are slow to dry out, and on some rough stony stretches in areas such as the Clwydian Hills.

The circular walks suggested at the ends of the sections are *not* part of the official national trail and may well not be signed or maintained to the same standard. You should be prepared to follow the map with great care when walking any of these.

Pleasures along the way

Having described the drawbacks, it is time to explain why, in spite of them, this Path is, as Lord Sandford said, the best. We have referred to the variety of landscape through which it passes, based on different geological formations, including hard sandstones and shales, limestone and the recent soft deposits of river flood plains. On the Black Mountains and the Clwydian Hills you can feel on top of the world, with views of more than 30 miles in every direction on a clear day. The low-land stretches have their views, too; not so wide-ranging, of course, but the Breidden Hills seen across the Severn, or the

The Severn Bridge from Sedbury Cliffs, at the southern end of the walk.

hills crowding in on the Wye Valley if you have chosen to follow the river, give you a detailed view of a contrasting landscape. No doubt you will feel an urge to explore these other hills laid out before you, and this is as it should be – in walking, as in other activities, one good thing leads to another.

The Offa's Dyke Path may have its own special and un-equalled beauties, but it also offers the walker a tantalising prospect of areas of countryside that are well worth visiting.

It is not just the distant views that will divert you from the

The Path above Bettws Dingle, a small wooded valley, north-east of Hay.

Path. Continually you will see or hear of buildings, historical and natural sites, or villages and small towns, within reach that you will want to visit. Though this book is divided into sections, each of which can be a comfortable day's walk between convenient stopping places, this arrangement is by no means the only way to walk the Path. It can be walked comfortably in about two weeks, but it is even better to allow extra time for some diversions – two hours for a walk down to Llanthony Abbey, half a day to see Denbigh, or even a day to climb Skirrid or the Breiddens.

This is also a splendid trail for the wildlife enthusiast with a little time to spare. Because of the variety of terrain covered by the Path, and its route through remote and sparsely populated country, a very wide range of species occurs. Recently compiled lists include up to 90 different birds, over 150 wild plant species (identified in a single day and a small area), 12 different butterflies and (in Radnorshire alone) 31 mammals, including nine species of bat, and eight amphibians or reptiles. Obviously we cannot list them all: some have been noted in the text to give local colour, particularly in relation to a season. We have taken care not to identify particular badger sites along the Path because of the problems with illegal hunting.

The Welsh Border has different beauties in each season: even winter is not very severe and the higher land to the west moderates the rainfall. Autumn colour is very fine and the moorlands when the heather is out are a special joy. Spring is a particularly good season to walk, for the variety of flowers then is especially wide, better views occur and birds are more easily seen before the trees are fully out.

This is a Path to linger over, and return to. There is a fine sense of achievement in arriving at Prestatyn seafront or Sedbury Cliffs, but the real pleasures are to be found on the way. Here you can understand why R. L. Stevenson could say, as he wandered through the Cevennes, in France, with a donkey to carry his pack (no stiles!): 'For my part, I travel not to go anywhere, but to go. I travel for travel's sake.'

PART TWO

OFFA'S DYKE PATH SOUTH
Chepstow to Knighton

The limestone cliffs of Wintour's Leap, seen from Lancaut. The Path runs on top of the cliffs.

1 Sedbury Cliffs to Monmouth

via Bigsweir and Redbrook
17½ miles (28 km)

This section of the Offa's Dyke Path follows the River Wye closely, for most of the way high up above the steep slopes of its eastern, English, side. The high route then follows the Dyke until this peters out at Redbrook. After that the Path diverges further from the Wye and climbs the Kymin, rejoining the river at Monmouth. Most of this part of the Path is within the Wye Valley Area of Outstanding Natural Beauty.

The southernmost end of the Dyke, and of the Path, is on the low cliffs overlooking the mudflats of the River Severn. Stand here **2**, turn your back on the earthwork and on the stone with its inscription about the path **1**. To the right is the Severn Bridge and its traffic (see page 45), ahead is Bristol and the whole of central and southern England, which the Dyke was meant to delimit. Turn again: in front of you stretches the Dyke, massive with a deep ditch to the south-west; and beyond are the suburbs of Chepstow. It is, however, one of the curious features of this Path that you cannot start walking it from its southern end. This can only be reached from the nearest road, then by walking quarter of a mile along a path that is the national trail.

Many south-to-north walkers will arrange to do the section south of Chepstow as an evening excursion from a base there, setting out on the sterner stuff further north next morning. There is now a very useful shortcut from the centre of Chepstow (and the station in particular) to the Offa's Dyke Path at Tutshill, as the railway bridge across the Severn at Buffer Wharf (see map) now has an adjacent new road and footway. A ramp takes you up to meet the Path on the B4228. Alternatively you may reach Sedbury by taking the frequent local Beachley bus from Chepstow to Buttington Tump **3**, a high ridge, possibly part of the Dyke, capped by a modern monolith but cut into by road works. Then walk 400 yards or so to the cliff top along the Path, and return to the road either by the same route or by the parallel path just south of Offa'a Dyke (to form a short *circuit*).

After this first stretch, the next mile or so, nearly all on the line of the Dyke, is walked only out of a sense of duty – over the trackway of the former railway to Beachley shipyards and through an extensive housing estate, complete with 'Offa's Close'! In 'Mercian Way' you walk in the ditch of the Dyke, and the bank above, on which sits the next tier of houses, actually is the earthwork.

After passing behind some newer houses, the Path joins the B4228, crosses the Chepstow bypass and the adjoining railway, and soon turns west on a surfaced path to follow behind older and more substantial houses. Below, to the west, is a magnificent view 4 over the Wye, with Rennie's 1816 bridge, towards Chepstow with its Norman castle. As a whimsy, on a stone wall just beneath the Path there is a stone model of the Severn Bridge with a menagerie of stone animals processing across one-by-one.

At a T-junction of paved paths is the way south to Chepstow (see feature on page 45), with the Path going northwards and soon crossing the former A48 Chepstow to Gloucester road at Tutshill. Cross fields, pass the ruins of the 16th century beacon of Tutshill Tower 5 and weave between drives and over more fields until an enclosed path takes you back to the B4228. Only 100 yards (90 metres) on this and then west again through a 19th century stone arch: 'Moyle Old School Lane' it says facing the road, but 'Mediaeval Times: Donkey Lane' on the back! At the top the view south gives a glorious panorama to the Severn Bridge.

The Path here runs above limestone cliffs, soon reaching Wintour's Leap 6, named after a Royalist leader said to have escaped his Parliamentary pursuers by leaping over the cliff. From here 7, the fine views extend south towards Chepstow, north-west towards the Lancaut peninsula and the Wye 200 feet (60 metres) below, possibly with rock climbers edging their way up towards you.

Some signs of Offa's Dyke are evident on the Lancaut peninsula with its ruined Norman church and Iron Age fort. Today's walker must walk along the B4228 and then along a stretch actually east of the road; an 'off-road' route, however, is likely before long (2000), so look out for waymarks. Notice a magnificent rabbit warren by the field edge just before you cross a series of stiles to regain the road again. At last, at Dennel Hill, it is west into the woods and soon north to follow a fine stretch of Dyke at the top of steeply wooded slopes down to the Wye. Although nearly all of the visible Dyke is protected as an ancient monument, English Heritage gives this stretch further protection with 'guardianship' status. The thick woodland partly conceals just how fine a stretch of Dyke this is. Badger enthusiasts will note the significance of the name 'Brockweir'.

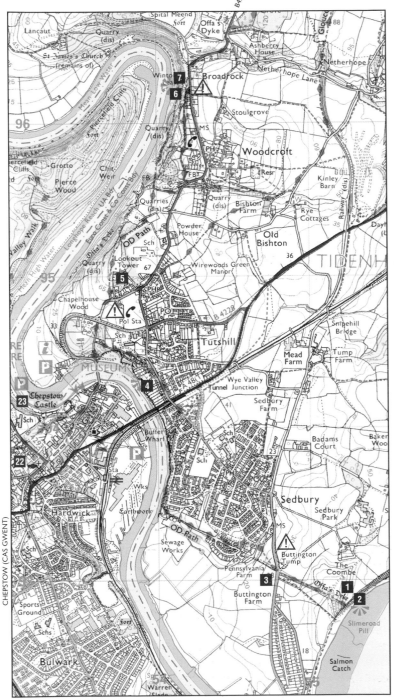

At **A** continue on a woodland path which turns onto a forestry track leading back to the earthwork. Take care to avoid a path descending towards the river **B**: your way follows the Dyke and, after a swing to the north, you are soon rewarded by a series of spectacular views over the Wye Valley. At the prominent Plumweir or Shorn Cliff rock you catch the first glimpse of the ruins of Tintern Abbey way beneath you **8**; then, in more open woods, you pass the memorial seat to Chris Pugh, for many years a Wye Valley warden, and reach the isolated limestone outcrop of the Devil's Pulpit **9** – a natural feature, but local legend has it that Old Nick preached from here to corrupt the monks of Tintern!

Continue in the ditch of the Dyke with the bank towering to the east – the Mercian side – and the (Welsh) Wye Valley below to the west. A path comes up from Tintern (see circular walk on page 43) just before you swing eastwards under the Dyke, the view down now being of Brockweir village and its bridge. Then the Dyke and Path descend to cross Brockweir side valley, at first gently, then leaving the ridge and dropping to the north with the Dyke as a shallow broad bank crossing a field. Over a stile by a gate you reach the edge of the Brockweir Valley and the only point on the whole Path where there is a choice between two official routes to follow. The riverside route (1) is a mile (1.6 km) longer than the one following the Dyke over the hills (2).

ROUTE 1: BY THE WYE

From the signpost marking the division of the routes, the 'low' way swings west along a broad bridleway past a horse rescue sanctuary and then north down Brockweir village street **10**. The inn and pottery are hospitable – and useful. The village has several Tudor houses, in particular the Manor House facing the bridge, and a church of the Moravian sect. Turn north along Quayside to follow the east bank of the river. Very soon a stile and footbridge are crossed and, if you have succeeded in picking a fine day, it is a gentle stroll by the riverside: hardly like a national trail! The beauties of the Wye can be appreciated **11**, usually with swans and signs of salmon and eels. This is one of the few stretches of the route open to horseriders, but in about a mile the footpath and bridleway diverge, the blue signs for the latter showing a route a little away from the river.

Pass Llandogo village on the opposite bank: when the river is low, rapids are evident. Continue below woods close to the water's edge to join the drive from St Briavels Hall, which

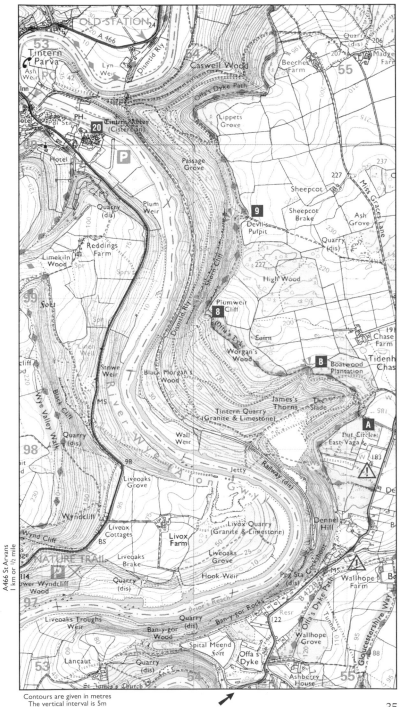

reaches the riverside through two prominent pillars. After 400 yards on the drive, continue on paths by the river to the east end of Bigsweir Bridge. This marks the highest tidal point on the river. A few yards east the high-level route joins up. Do not expect facilities at Bigsweir – just a bus stop on the A466.

ROUTE 2: BY ST BRIAVELS COMMON

This follows the line of the Dyke, here very fragmented, through the scattered dwellings of St Briavels Common and the Hudnalls, and it must be followed with great care **C**. From the signpost marking the division of the routes, descend the field with the Dyke and later with a wood to the south; note the abundance of foxgloves on the bank leading to the footbridge over the Brockweir brook. Rise to a stile on to the Brockweir to Hewelsfield road and go east on it, then very quickly north away from it. Cross a small footbridge and rise to the Cold-harbour road, where a rapid left and right gains an enclosed path, emerging on a road in the same northerly direction. At a fork by Two Springs take the higher, easterly, option. Pass a converted chapel and rise, with Offa's Dyke, on an enclosed path. Take the westerly fork near the top and at the brow go left, then half right, respecting the 'private property' notice in traversing the paddocks belonging to The Fields, via a series of four stiles.

Reach a road, turn north and where, in 200 yards, this swings east, continue along the unsurfaced lane (by the 'Oak Cottage' sign) to 'Sittingreen' where the road swings east to Birchfield House, distinguished by some fine pine trees and the first view on this stretch **12** of the Wye Valley and Bigsweir Bridge. After 150 yards turn north down a confined path. This enters a scarp-bank wood, zigzagging steeply, and is certainly no place to race, particularly when it is wet: the apparently short flight of steps turn out to be fretted planks, to be negotiated with great caution **D**. At the bottom of the wood cross two fields downhill, aiming for a stone bridge and a cattle grid on the access drive to Bigsweir House and follow this to the bridge on the A466 just east of where the river bank route emerges.

Routes 1 and 2 above combine to form an attractive 6.4-mile (10.1-km) *circuit*. Tintern Old Station (see page 43) provides nearby parking.

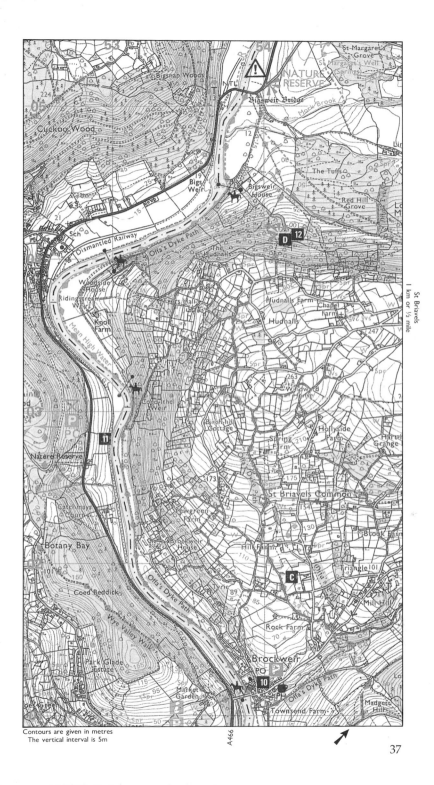

Contours are given in metres
The vertical interval is 5m

A466

St Briavels
1 km or ½ mile

37

After Bigsweir the walker stays on the A466 for a few yards before taking the fork to St Briavels. Follow this uphill to the point where a lane joins on the left. Here a path leads off into the woodland which now starts on the lefthand side of the road. This path runs inside the wood roughly parallel with the road before turning north, making a zig-zag crossing of the Dyke and continuing northwards, climbing to re-cross the Dyke nearly 300 feet up it, and then following it before descending again through Creeping Hill Wood.

Many walkers may, however, choose to continue along the St Briavels' road to the little hill village whose 13th century castle of the Warden of the Forest of Dean is now a comfortable youth hostel **13**. In order to rejoin the Path from St Briavels, retrace your steps along the road to the point where you crossed the Dyke, just past the last house, and turn right on a small lane running northwards. Continue on this past a Woodland Trust sign (there are waymarked walks from here **14**) and then take a path north into the woods opposite two white houses. You will join the main Path about 100 yards before it crosses the Dyke near the top of the hill.

The next stretch is through fields at the top of a steep bank of woodland down to the Wye, glimpsed as you look south to Bigsweir. The Dyke forms the top edge of the wood. Through a small plantation and the Dyke is once more a clear boundary above as you approach remote Coxbury Farm. Beyond the buildings the Path – and Dyke   turns upwards and crosses a muddy lane to regain the high bank, with woods steeply below, on Highbury Plains. In a curious stretch the Dyke, after a reverse S-bend to gain the ridge from the farm, is now on the lower of two parallel banks, the one that commands the slope down to the river. There is evidence of small-scale quarrying, probably for walling and roof tiles. After three-quarters of a mile Highbury Farm is reached and the Dyke, your companion for most of the past 14 miles (22.5 km) is with you no more and you will not meet it again for another 54 miles (87 km)!

Past the oddly battlemented buildings of this hill farm, the Path slopes steeply down two fields towards Redbrook, with yet another of the splendid views of the Wye **15**, crossed at the village by the old railway bridge. At the bottom the way is clear though there is an unavoidable flight of 67 steps to be negotiated! Redbrook **16** (see feature on ironworking on page 48) is a 19th century industrial village on the valley road, the A466, perhaps the only village with three pubs, all with four-letter names, all beginning with the letter 'B'?

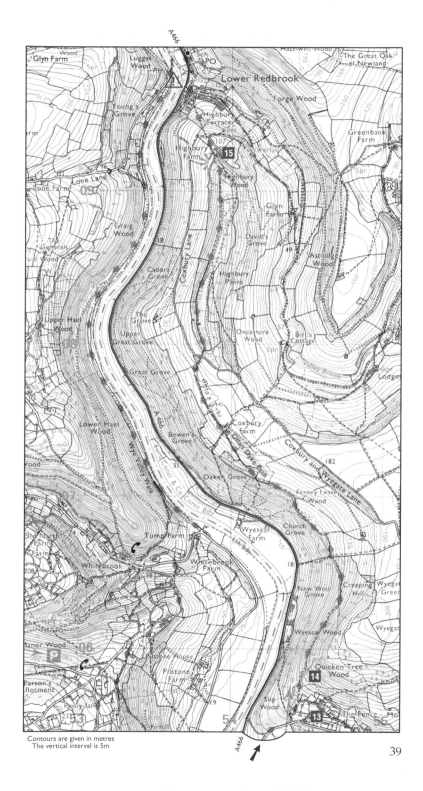

Contours are given in metres
The vertical interval is 5m

39

Pass through Redbrook to the Little Chef and garage: here follow the rising lane opposite, diverging away from the pavement of the main road, with a view upriver beyond the Bush Inn. The lane leads between houses to join the B4231 Newland road at the foot of an old colliery incline by a ruined mill. Walk up the road for nearly 400 yards past other remains of the valley's industrial past. Hopefully the route may one day be changed here to take walkers off this busy road.

Fork north, away from the road, behind a cottage; at the top of the steep rise the track turns sharply north into a wide hollow-way (a path through a cutting) past Duffield's Farm. Press on up the track, Duffield's Lane, to Cockshoot Ash Barn. There the Path goes off diagonally north-eastwards over a fence stile and rises to a further one. Then walk above the wooded scarp to a kissing gate and an access path to the Kymin (National Trust) **17**.

Go along the path at the western edge of the car park to reach both the Naval Temple and the Round House viewpoint **18** (see page 49). Blessed with good visibility, this is one of the most exciting prospects on the whole Dyke Path, with Monmouth and the Wye in front, the mid-Monnow and Trothy hill country – through which the Path threads – in the middle ground, and a backcloth of the Black Mountains with Blorenge and Skirrid Fawr, partly shielding Sugar Loaf. From Monmouth the Round House crowns the view of the slopes of the Kymin; on a fine day its white painted walls shine resplendently.

Continuing north past a garage, the Path descends to the west on a short flight of stone steps and soon slants down beside a conifer plantation to join briefly a drive, adjacent to Rose Tree Cottage. Continue across a stile and steeply down the roughly bracken-clad pasture to enter Garth Wood, swinging west on a clear path on a shelf in the trees. At the foot of the wood, join the Kymin road as it proceeds downhill. Where this bends north, continue forward through two kissing gates on to a narrow path which runs above and then joins the A4136. At the May Hill Inn cross the road to follow the pavement to the Wye Bridge and the subway under the heavy traffic of the A40, the Monmouth bypass. There is more than 700 feet (over 200 metres) difference in height between here and the top of the Kymin.

Starting points of the half-day walks that follow can be reached by Monmouth to Chepstow buses. See also page 36 for a third walk.

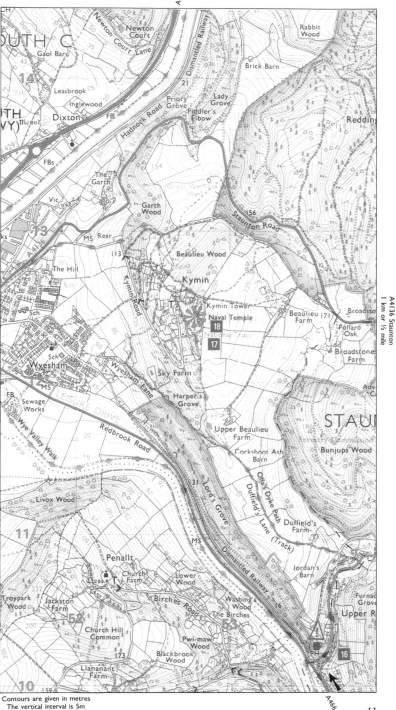

A40

Newton Court Lane

Rabbit Wood

Gaol Barn

Dismantled Railway

Brick Barn

14

Leasbrook

25

Priory Grove

Lady Grove

Redding

Inglewood

Dixton

FB

Fiddler's Elbow

Hadnock Road

21

The Garth

154

Great Warren

Vic

Garth Wood

Staunton Road

156

MS Resr

113

Beaulieu Wood

The Hill

Kymin

Kymin Road

A4136 Staunton
1 km or ½ mile

Kymin Tower

Beaulieu Farm

171

Broadsto

Sch

Naval Temple

18

Pollard Oak

17

National Trust

Broadstones Farm

Wyesham

Sch

Sky Farm

Ady

Harper's Grove

Wyesham Lane

C

STAUI

FB

LEISURE DRIVE

Upper Beaulieu Farm

Sewage Works

Redbrook Road

20

Corkshoot Ash Barn

Bunjups Wood

Wye Valley Walk

Forestry Commission

Livox Wood

31

Lord's Grove

Offa's Dyke Path

Duffield's Lane (Track)

Duffield's Farm

11

MS

Dismantled Railway

Jordan's Barn

Penallt

Church Farm

Lower Wood

Cross

Troypark Wood

Jackston Farm

Birches Road

Washing's Wood

16

Furnac Grove

52

The Birches

Upper R

Church Hill Common

Pwll-maw Wood

173

Blackbrook Wood

PH

16

Llananant Farm

10

159

A466

Contours are given in metres
The vertical interval is 5m

41

The Path through Shorn Cliff woods, high above the Wye Valley.

Contours are given in metres
The vertical interval is 5m

A CIRCULAR WALK VIA THE DEVIL'S PULPIT
3 or 4½ miles (4.8 or 7.3 km)

The Tintern Old Station picnic site (grid ref. 536 005) has car parking available. The site retains its station buildings with buffet, toilets and exhibition room, the signal box used as an information centre and other minor railway fittings, including a grand set of signals **19**.

Follow the old railway track north to steps on to Brockweir Bridge. Turn east over the bridge to join the riverside option of the Offa's Dyke Path, and go through Brockweir to meet Offa's Dyke at the junction of the two alternative official Paths.

Turn south on the Offa's Dyke Path, initially uphill in a sunken lane, and continue on it for about a mile, generally on the west side of the Dyke (described in the opposite direction on page 34). The Monk's Passage, a signposted path leading down towards Tintern, can be followed for the short walk, but to see the best of the views over the Wye Valley continue upwards on the Path for another three-quarters of a mile past the limestone pinnacle of the Devil's Pulpit to the Plumweir/Shorn Cliff view-point **8** (see map on page 35) for the open prospect over Tintern Abbey in its beautiful valley setting. A common phenomenon of these woodlands flanking the Wye Valley is their capacity to create localised cloud, which materialises, swirls and evaporates in the twinkling of an eye.

Return to the head of the Monk's Passage and follow the 'Tintern' sign down to a forestry track. Go right and soon left on to a narrow path (watch your step in negotiating the rocky cleft **E**), sweeping down to join a bridleway coming in from Brockweir (to the north). Continue down the hollow-way left and at the foot of the cobbled incline (see page 48 on ironworking) slip through the metal barrier posts. From here there is a fine view to Tintern Abbey across the river. Cross the Wireworks Bridge into Tintern village, going left to visit the abbey **20** (see page 48).

The circuit is completed by going north along the pavement of the A466 for half a mile. Then, opposite the Catbrook turn, take a narrow lane signposted 'Wye Valley Walk/St Michael's Church', passing behind Parva Farmhouse and through the churchyard. Follow the river bank by stiles to reach the old railway bridge abutment at Lyn Weir and climb the steps to reach the Old Station along the former track.

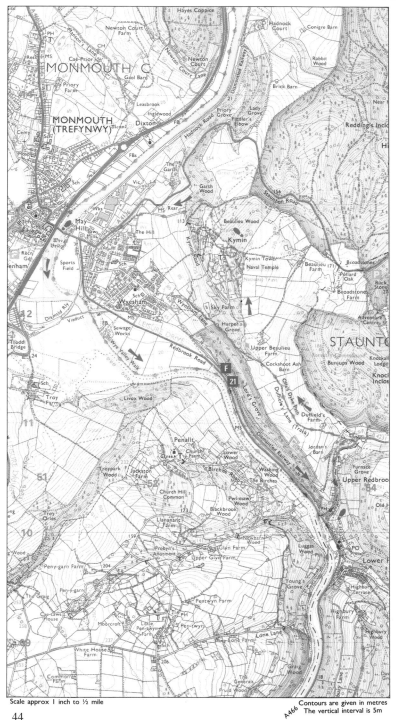

Contours are given in metres
The vertical interval is 5m

A466

A CIRCULAR WALK TO KYMIN
5½ miles (8.8 km)

Cars can be parked off the A466 at Redbrook (grid ref. 536 101). Alternatively, the circuit can be walked from car parks at Monmouth or Kymin. Follow the official Offa's Dyke Path over the Kymin to the east side of the Wye Bridge at Monmouth as described on page 40. Turn south on the riverside route waymarked as the 'Wye Valley Walk', part of a joint county council initiative for a route from Chepstow, mostly along the Wye to Hereford, Hay-on-Wye, Builth Wells and Rhayader.

On the riverside path keep to the river side of the sports grounds to a disused railway bridge crossing the river and the remains of a viaduct; continue on a steep and narrow path past a sewage works into fields beside the river. The views across the Wye are delightful **21**. In 1½ miles (about 2.5 km) there is another narrow, often muddy and slippery stretch through bushes below the A466 **F**. The path then widens again and eventually takes you out on to this main road just north of Redbrook. However, opposite the Bush Inn another stile takes you back to the river bank for a further short stretch before returning beside a football pitch to the road in Redbrook village.

Severn Bridge

This was designed by Sir Gilbert Roberts and opened in 1966. Its advanced engineering features made it lighter and cheaper than the Forth Road Bridge opened two years earlier. With its tall openwork towers and slender suspension cables, it is a striking but graceful feature in the view from the Offa's Dyke Path from Sedbury and for some distance to the north.

Chepstow **22**

Although the Dyke and the Path are on the east side of the River Wye here, Chepstow is regarded by many as the southern terminus of an Offa's Dyke walk. It is the place you can reach by train or coach and its accommodation ranges from simple guest houses to luxury hotels. The town is so interesting that only extreme shortage of time can justify omission of a visit!

The main street runs down through Beaufort Square to the river, but is not straight, so the view is limited at any point by

Chepstow with its castle, seen from the Path.

the corners of buildings of many periods. Near the top the street is spanned by the Town Gate, rebuilt in 1524, part of the 12th century Port Wall, much of which survives to a great height with seven of its original 10 projecting towers.

Following the wall down northwards from the gate to the Castle Dell, you soon reach the castle itself **23**. It is in the care of Cadw, Welsh Historic Monuments (see page 138), is open all the year, and entrance is through the great gatehouse at the lower, eastern end. Because of its situation on a narrow spur running down to the Wye, its four courtyards are set end to end: Lower, Middle and Upper Baileys, beyond which a narrow passage alongside the Great Tower leads to the fourth and highest courtyard, the Barbican. The earliest parts date from 1067, just after the Norman Conquest, but mostly it is 13th century.

St Mary's Church retains from its Norman foundation a fine west doorway and font, but it was heavily restored in the 19th century. The museum and Information Centre near the castle entrance, and many buildings in the town, are worth inspection.

Ironworking in the Wye Valley

The Forest of Dean became established as a major ironworking area, using local ore, in the 17th century, utilising the River Wye as a transport highway and the swift streams descending its steep eastern slopes for power.

Tintern was an industrial metal-working settlement in the 17th and 18th centuries and the wireworks survived until the late 19th century. What now remains is the bridge across the river which once carried the tramway serving the works. Your circuit route from the Path to Tintern uses the bridge and part of the old tramway route.

A string of ponds in the Lower Redbrook Valley, which once worked the furnaces and forges, still survives. Here and at Upper Redbrook there are remains of the mills and other industrial structures, including the inclined plane crossing the B4231.

Tintern Abbey **20**

The abbey is owned and managed by Cadw and open to visitors all the year. A visit outside the main season, when there are no crowds, is a haunting experience. In its superb riverside setting the abbey is more beautiful as a ruin than we can ever imagine it being in its complete state.

Founded in 1131, for monks of the Cistercian Order, it was largely rebuilt in the 13th century, the church entirely so. This, though roofless, is still almost complete, with delicate window tracery in the Decorated style, especially in the exquisite great west window. On the north side of the church are the magnificent 15th century cloisters, leading to the buildings associated with the business, study and everyday life of the monks and lay brothers – the Chapter House, parlour, dormitories and refectories.

The Kymin **17**

The two strange buildings on the summit were both built by the 'Gentlemen of the Kymin Club', a late 18th century dining club. The battlemented Round House, of 1794, contained a kitchen and banquet room. In 1800 the Naval Temple was added. They have recently been restored by the National Trust to much of their former glory, including the replacement of the statue of Britannia on top of the Temple. The Temple celebrates the naval victories of the period, especially those of Nelson who, along with Sir William and Emma Hamilton, visited the site – for a public breakfast! – in 1802 and is recorded as being impressed by the monument and the view.

The late 18th century Round House on the Kymin.

The 13th century gatehouse situated on the Monnow Bridge in Monmouth.

2 Monmouth to Pandy

through Llantillio Crossenny and past White Castle
16¾ miles (27 km)

There is no waymarked route for the mile through Monmouth but the following walk is attractive and gives you the chance to 'see the sights' and sample the facilities. After crossing the Wye Bridge and using the underpass under the A40, go up Wyebridge Street opposite, then left (south) and immediately right into St Mary's Street. This brings you out opposite the church. Go south here along the pedestrianised Church Street and then down the full length of the historic main street. At the bottom cross the Monnow by the gatehoused bridge and turn west into Drybridge Street. One-third of a mile further on, opposite the end of a recreation ground, the Path resumes its westward route along Watery Lane.

The next 16 miles (26 km) to Pandy are largely in the valley of the River Trothy, a tributary of the Wye, which it joins just south of Monmouth. The country is pleasant though unexciting farmland, and care is needed as the route passes over a succession of fields and minor roads. The villages and churches, plus White Castle, are the joys. There is no Offa's Dyke to be seen: fragmentary sections of what may be the earthwork are found further up the Wye Valley north of Monmouth but the Path walker will not rejoin it until beyond Kington (page 110).

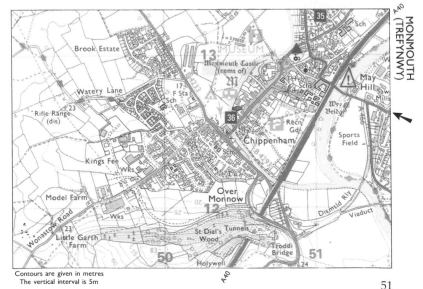

Contours are given in metres
The vertical interval is 5m

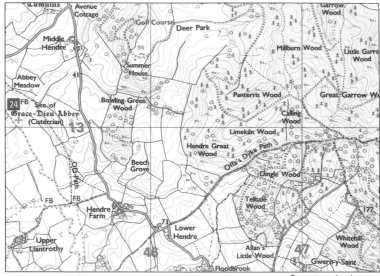

Contours are given in metres
The vertical interval is 5m

From the Monmouth end of Watery Lane there is a further mile along the road before your next field walking (*see map on page 53, continuing above*). At first there are estates, then the houses become more spaced and the stream beside the road – 'Watery' Lane – is pleasant. Looking south towards Monmouth the Kymin stands out. At the sharp turn of the road south-west to Bailey Pits Farm, you swing into a field and keep to its north edge with the stream now on the other side of the hedge. After two fields and two footbridges, the latter over a deep gully, you climb steeply westwards through the coverts of King's Wood, and you may see deer tracks. In the early days of walking the Path, this was one of the boggiest, most frustrating parts of the route and the 'dreaded Bailey Pits' **A** were notorious among walkers. The going is now much easier, thanks to Gwent County Council's fine waymarking and bridging job. A proposed golf course here will lead to further changes in the landscape.

Just before the watershed at the top of the climb in King's Wood, a boundary stone marked '1857 Monmouth' is passed and now it is all downhill on a clear forestry track to the road at Lower Hendre Farm.

Turn north-west along this minor road for quarter of a mile, pass the fine Hendre Farmhouse, then turn west across a stile immediately beyond a new house (not marked on the map). Over the brow of a rise you see the River Trothy below you for

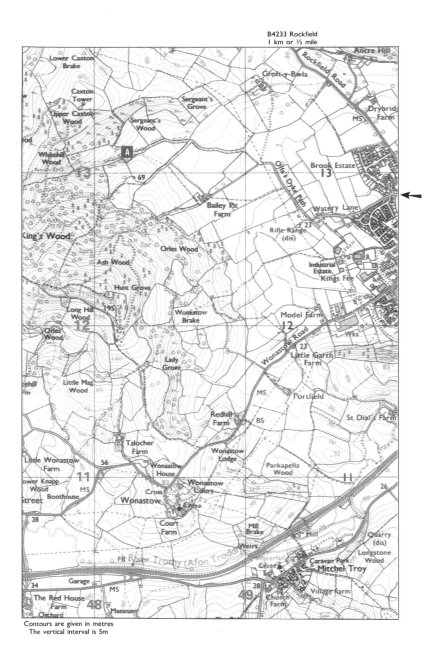

Contours are given in metres
The vertical interval is 5m

the first time. The route crosses a footbridge and then lies a little
above its east bank. Between you and the river there is the site of
the 13th century Cistercian Grace Dieu Abbey **24**; but not a stone
is to be seen now. Going west along the next road reached,
however, you cross 'Abbey' Bridge.

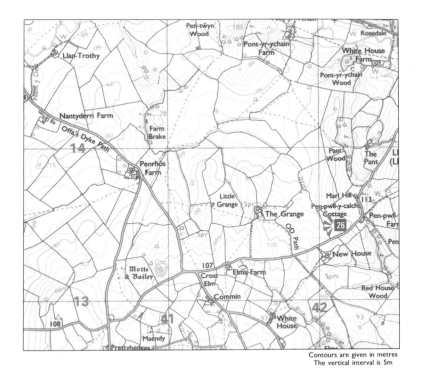

Contours are given in metres
The vertical interval is 5m

Very soon after the bridge the north-west direction is resumed, but this time in the fields west of the river (*see map on page 55, continuing above*). Four fields on, a steep path down soon brings you near the river bank itself. Follow this westwards to just under Sunnybank. Join the drive of this house and you will reach the isolated medieval church of Llanvihangel-Ystern-Llewern (St Michael's of the Fiery Meteor) **25**. The churchyard is well kept and the porch inviting for a rest, but remember that the cost of upkeep in such a sparsely populated area is difficult to meet, so any donation you can give will be appreciated. Take the narrow path at the end of the churchyard beside a tributary stream, or skirt round the north side of the church to it.

Swing west and up to cross a drive, and then a long climb up fields leads to the next road by the farm of Pen-pwll-y-calch, and a one-third of a mile walk westwards along the road. Here **26**, note the shapes of Skirrid and Sugar Loaf to the north: they will dominate the views ahead. Leave the road by a stile on its north side and circle a large field anti-clockwise before crossing a horse training area and the drive of The Grange; please keep to the Path here. Descend through several fields to another minor road.

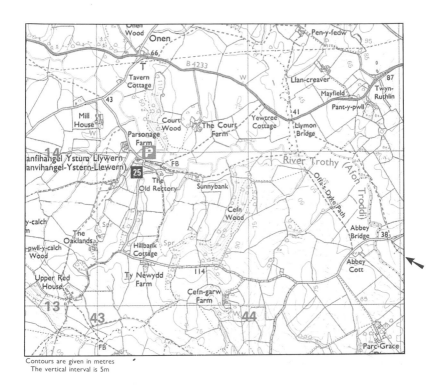

Contours are given in metres
The vertical interval is 5m

Storm clouds over Skirrid, seen from Great Treadam.

Follow the road for a mile north-westwards into Llantilio Crossenny village, the largest and most interesting on this part of the route. It has a fine, large, 13th century church **27** dedicated to St Teilo, 6th century Bishop of Llandaff, which is the venue for a splendid annual music festival in early May. The village inn, The Hostry **28**, has features dating from 1459 and a collection of local curios.

The route goes through a kissing gate immediately after crossing the Trothy. Two fields on, a further kissing gate takes you out on to a second road. The church is to the north-east but the route goes south-west along the road towards the inn. Before it, however, turn north-west through another kissing gate, and then yet another one to the B4233. Cross this and start to climb westwards over a series of fields. However, a short diversion east along the B road to the site of Hen Cwrt (the Old Court) **29**, of which only the moat remains, is suggested first. It is open to visitors.

In half a mile (800 metres), at the top of the slopes, you reach and then pass south-west of a group of pretty ponds before joining Great Treadam farm road just before this large house.

The 13th century church of St Teilo at Llantilio Crossenny.

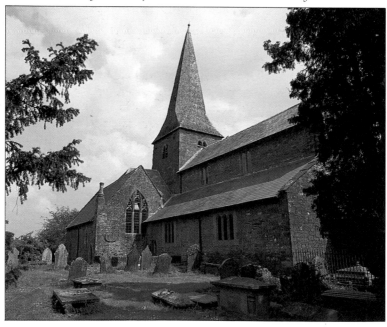

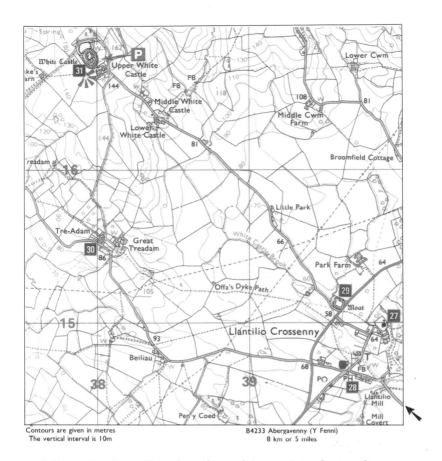

Contours are given in metres
The vertical interval is 10m

B4233 Abergavenny (Y Fenni)
8 km or 5 miles

Follow the Great Treadam farm drive out to the road; go a
few yards north-west along this, and turn north again by Old
Treadam **30**. This house, dating from 1600, is worth more than a
casual glance as you pass by. A three-quarter mile (1 km) climb
along an enclosed surfaced lane brings you to the road just
below White Castle **31**. Looking south-east, most of the route
you have followed (or will take if going south) from Monmouth
can be made out and the Kymin beyond is clear. The castle is of
course not to be missed (see page 64).

It was a happy thought to route the Path on the track round
the northern two-thirds of the castle, since it gives a splendid
chance to appreciate it from a range of aspects. The hill crowned
by the castle can also be picked out on the Path from some
distance to the north. The Path then drops south-west on a field
edge to Duke's Barn and then through 90 degrees to fall steeply
north-west to cross a river – it *is* the Trothy again. Swing north

57

The churchyard of St Cadoc's at Llangattock-lingoed, with summer meadow flowers.

just after the bridge and along the eastern edge of two fields to reach the B4521 between Llanvetherine and Caggle Street hamlets.

Turn north-east on the road for 300 yards and then, just past a chapel, climb north-westwards again over a series of fields. Farm buildings are reached at a hollow-way near the top of a rise and the route turns again, this time north along the hollow-way. Route-finding over this stretch is not easy but the waymarking is good **B**. Soon you will pass the fine farm and outbuildings of Little Pool Hall to your right, noting, alas, that this is now no longer lived in, and then you go down a field to a footbridge and out to a minor road. Here there is a sign to the inn at Llangattock-lingoed but you have nearly a mile to go. Much of the distance is on this little road: halfway along note the Jacobean farmhouse at Old Court where you take the 'No Through Road' ahead.

The road beyond Old Court passes Cwm Farm, on the left (west). Opposite this go down a steep track, over a footbridge (the Full Brook, an aptly named Trothy tributary) and then a subsidiary stream. Then up a (very) steep field to St Cadoc's Churchyard at Llangattock-lingoed **32**. Both the church and the Hunter's Moon Inn, to the east, have 13th century features.

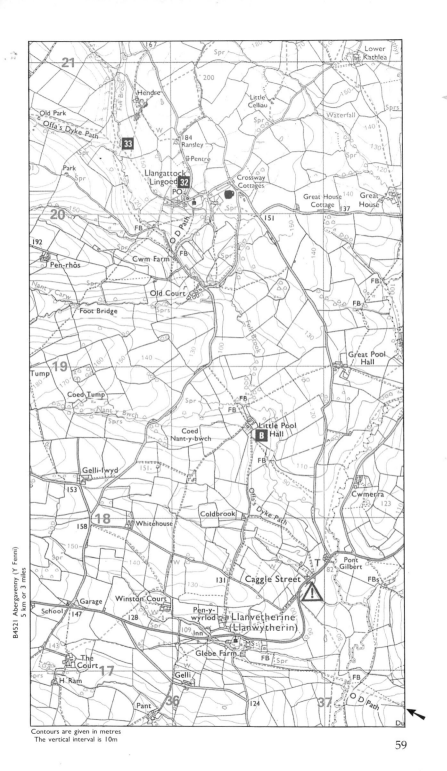

Contours are given in metres
The vertical interval is 10m

B4521 Abergavenny (Y Fenni)
5 km or 3 miles

Walk along the road away from the inn and up steps beyond the former school to reach fields with the Full Brook Valley below on your left (south-west). Drop to near its confluence with a smaller stream, cross a bridge and rise on the col between the two valleys. In a minor way this is both a beautiful and spectacular spot 33. Follow the Path above the stream and eventually drop to its bank to reach a road at an often muddy point C. Cross the river (this is the last you will see of the Trothy and its tributaries, your companions for 11 miles/18 km) and walk up fields to reach and follow Llanerch Farm drive.

The drive soon reaches a small road. Turn right (north-west) to reach a T-junction in 100 yards, then left (south-west) for a similar stretch. The Path then takes to the fields for a mile, going north-west across and generally down a series of fields: there are many stiles, some doubled to cross ditches, and a careful watch to pick up the next stile and waymark on the route is essential D. The Honddu Valley you are aiming for is always below you with a fine panorama 34 of the Black Mountains ridges that you will soon be following. Eventually you reach a farm track. Go west along this to the busy A465 (Hereford to Abergavenny) opposite the Lancaster Arms at Pandy. This is the first spot on the Path since leaving Monmouth with a regular daily bus route: the next one is Hay-on-Wye – a further very long day's walk ahead.

THREE CASTLES WALK
19 miles (30.6 km)

Gwent County Council has established a splendid two-day walk linking the 'Trilateral' of Skenfrith, White and Grosmont Castles (see page 64) through the picturesque and little-known country of northern Gwent. From White Castle 31 the route heads north, traversing Graig Syfyrddin via Edmund's Tump to reach Grosmont, from where it wanders downstream within the beautiful Monnow Valley to Skenfrith (starting point of Gwent County Council's guide). From here the route wends west-south-west to regain the Path. It is a fascinating walk of real quality. For further details of this route, together with the Wye Valley Walk and other waymarked routes and guided walks in the county, contact Gwent County Council, Planning Department, County Hall, Cwmbran, NP44 2XH.

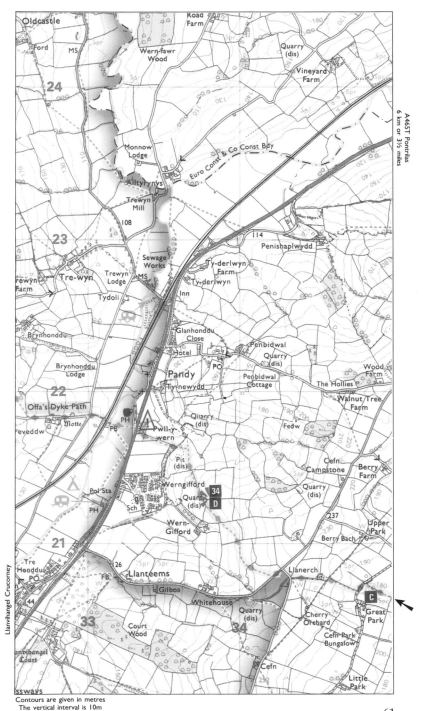

Contours are given in metres
The vertical interval is 10m

61

White Castle, mainly 12th century, with its water-filled moat.

Three Castles

The three castles of the 'Trilateral', White, Skenfrith and Grosmont, were built by Norman Marcher lords to defend the route from Monmouth into Wales. White Castle **31**, now bereft of any village surroundings, is the most impressive of the three – a late 12th century curtain wall surrounding an inner ward with drum towers at the angles added in refortification during the Border warfare of the 13th century. Though roofless, all the walls are almost intact and are still surrounded by a watery moat, now often the home of waterfowl. In bright weather this is every child's idea of a toy castle – but at full size; when it is dull, however, it becomes once more the threatening fortress of the Middle Ages. This place, memorable to visit at all times, is in the care of Cadw. The castle has little later history, but a curious recent episode was a number of visits by Hitler's deputy, Rudolf Hess, who was for a time a captive at nearby Maindiff Court.

A visit to the other two castles is strongly recommended. Skenfrith lies in a pretty setting by the Monnow in the heart of a small village. Grosmont is also in a village (with a shop!) which retains its medieval borough features, with a minuscule town hall in the square. You can visit these castles by following part or all of the 'Castles Alternative' to the Offa's Dyke trail between Monmouth and Hay-on-Wye (details from Offa's Dyke Association, see page 139) or by use of the Gwent County Council circular route linking the three castles (see page 60).

Monmouth

The largest town directly on the Path apart from Prestatyn, Monmouth **35** (see map, page 51) is also full of historical interest. No doubt its most famous feature is the 13th century gatehouse **36** on the bridge over the Monnow, the only one of its kind in Britain, and in perfect repair, in contrast to the fragmentary ruins of the castle. This is on the site of a Norman motte and bailey, but the remains now visible are of the 12th century Great Tower with additions from the 14th and 15th centuries. The future Henry V was born here in 1387: his statue is one of two to be seen in the suitably named Agincourt Square. The other is of Charles Rolls, pioneer of aviation and joint founder of the Rolls-Royce car and aero-engine firm. In the square is the fine Georgian Shire Hall with an open area reached through arches at ground level, often occupied by market stalls.

Between the square and Monnow Bridge, the main shopping area, Monnow Street, runs for one-third of a mile, with many interesting buildings (look above the ground-floor level) and historical remains below ground, which current excavations are revealing. Above Agincourt Square the road divides, Priory Street leading in a short distance to the interesting museum (Nelson upstairs, local history below). Between this and the castle is Great Castle House, of 1673, now occupied by the military but sometimes open to the public. Further up Priory Street, the 15th century remains of the priory have been incorporated in later buildings. Here lived Geoffrey of Monmouth, the famous 12th century chronicler, whose purported histories include tales of King Arthur.

The narrow way out of Agincourt Square, Church Street, leads to St Mary's Church, rebuilt in 1881–2 apart from the 14th century tower with its graceful 18th century spire, and beyond to St James's Square with a famous and beautiful catalpa tree. There are two other churches with medieval work, St Peter at Dixton, a little way north-east by the Wye, and St Thomas, just over the old bridge at Over Monnow – an early industrial centre (knitting!) surrounded by its own, probably Norman, defensive ditch, the Clawdd Ddu (Black Dyke).

3 Pandy to Hay-on-Wye

along Hatterrall Hill and past Hay Bluff
17½ miles (28.2 km)

Pandy marks a landmark in the route: the next stretch of Offa's Dyke Path is not through farmland and by rivers, but on the Black Mountains, and the Hatterrall Ridge in particular. The route on the Hatterrall Ridge is in the main along the border of England and Wales and also on the eastern boundary of the Brecon Beacons National Park, who help to manage this part of the Path. You must decide whether to walk the stretch in one day. If you do, then you need to be fit and to have a fine day. If you are more cautious you can find accommodation at Llanthony (or Capel-y-ffin) on the west (see map on page 77) or Longtown on the east (see page 80 for link route) – about 2 miles (just over 3 km) away in each case, but the routes and the destinations are spectacular (see page 82).

Cross a stile just south of the Lancaster Arms on the by-road leading off the main A465. Soon a footbridge crosses the Honddu and then, between a pair of kissing gates, take care in going across the busy Newport to Hereford railway. Before reaching a minor road, note the castle mound across the hedge to the west. Continue forward on this road to pass the large farm of Treveddw and soon afterwards cut off a corner of the road by ascending a large field diagonally in a northerly direction to a converted barn. Go along the road again for half a mile; halfway along you go round a right-angled bend and continue down and *east*! This seems perverse since soon you have a steep climb north-west but, to compensate, do admire the view **37** across the valley to the Skirrid range which dominated the stretch of Path further south.

Look for a steep hollow-way leading you from the road to the open ridges. At its top there is an entirely different, moorland, scene. First make for the west edge of a clump of pines above you, at the south corner of the fine Pentwyn Iron Age hill fort **38**. The Path goes across the middle of the fort and emerges at its northern corner. This is one point **A** where the correct route can be missed, as there are several paths forward and it is little use asking the mountain sheep you are sure to see hereabouts. Make for the east edge of a large walled enclosure you will note ahead, usually known as 'The Castle'. Beyond this the way is clear, steep and without obvious alternatives.

Longtown
2 km or 1 mile

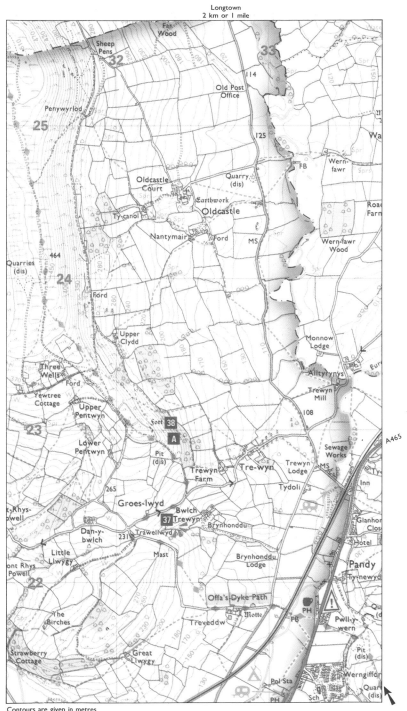

Contours are given in metres
The vertical interval is 10m

The immediate objective of the climb is the trig point at the first summit at 1,521 feet (464 metres). The views into the two valleys at either side begin to open out and are seen to even better advantage when the route swings a little west to near the summit of Hatterrall Hill itself (1,743 feet/531 metres). There is a gentle drop from here and, on anything like a clear day, Llanthony Abbey (or Priory) in the Honddu Valley to the west and Longtown in the Olchon to the east will shine out (see circular walk on page 75 and link route on page 80).

We have seen this area in many moods and seasons but, on one particular February day in a near-blizzard, we were rewarded by a sudden clearance which bathed Llanthony in sunshine 39: one of those moments to be treasured. Beyond you will see the higher hills that are next on the agenda, but before them, at the foot of the small drop, you reach a cross path (grid ref. 307 270). This is less than 5 miles (8 km) from Pandy and the best point to drop to Llanthony or Longtown if weather or fatigue makes you decide to split the Black Mountains traverse.

The next 7 miles (11.2 km) call for far less comment. You are walking a little west of north, following the English–Welsh border, as you gradually climb the long ridge leading from the top of Hatterrall Hill. This gets increasingly wide, obscuring the views to east and west as it does so. In addition, as the ridge widens the surface deteriorates, with less stone and more peat to walk on. The pressure of 20 years of walkers breaking through the thin soil has inevitably contributed to this, and those determined to keep dry boots and feet play an interesting game of 'diversions', competing to see just how little extra distance they need to add in avoiding the worst of the wet patches B. From a hang glider, and there are many to be seen here, the antics of walkers playing this game must be amusing.

How you view this section is a matter of individual temperament – and the season and weather. In August it is a mass of heather and bilberry, and in a dry spell the peat hags are no problem; but in wet or misty weather the chief joy must be in overcoming the conditions – and dangers. Despite the heavy use of the Path, poor visibility can make you lose your way, and though the top of the ridge is flat the edges are precipitous. In such conditions it is best to drop down the path to Llanthony 40 and continue up the Honddu Valley road to and beyond Capel-y-ffin 41 (see pages 71 and 82). The Path is then rejoined where it reaches the road a mile or so north of the Gospel Pass (see map on page 73).

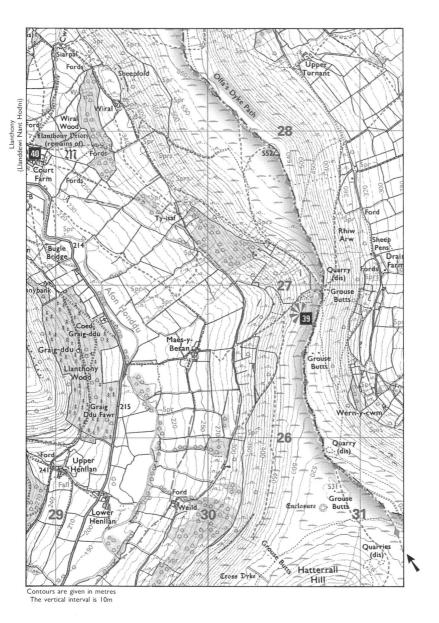

Contours are given in metres
The vertical interval is 10m

You will see groups of ponies grazing and probably also organised parties of pony trekkers; the last time we walked this stretch we even saw cycle tyre marks the whole way, but the owner must have been trying to prove something. The Offa's Dyke Path itself, however, is not a bridleway here, and it is illegal to cycle or ride on a footpath.

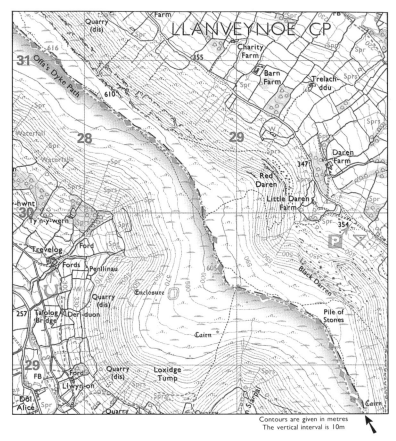

Contours are given in metres
The vertical interval is 10m

A few landmarks do signify points of progress. There is an Ordnance Survey trig point, less than a mile north of the Llanthony to Longtown cross path, at 1,810 feet (552 metres), and then a fainter cross path leading back to Llanthony westwards and steeply north-east to a small car park under Black Darren. A series of cairns begins to mark the route and each conscientious walker usually adds a stone. Less than 3 miles (5 km) further on you reach another trig point at 2,010 feet (610 metres) and then a further faint cross path to Capel-y-ffin (west) and the upper Olchon Valley (east) (see circular walk on page 85). From here **42** the ridge to the east, the Cat's Back and Black Hill (used by this circuit), looks fine and, to the south, the edge of the ridge you are walking on, Red Daren, looks more spectacular than seems possible when you are actually on top of it. You gradually ascend to the top of the ridge, at 2,306 feet (703 metres). This is the highest point on the whole Path!

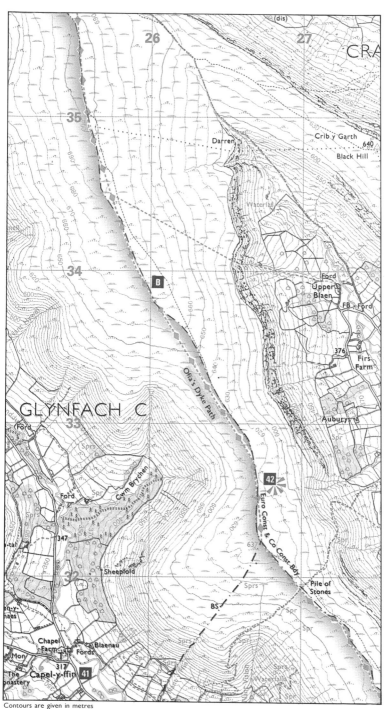

26 27 CRA

(dis)

35 Darren Crib y Garth 640
Black Hill 600

Waterfall 550

500

34 Ford 450
B Upper Blaen
FB Ford

376 Firs Farm

Olfa's Dyke Path

GLYNFACH C Auburys
33 (Ford) Spr

Spr Cwm Brychan

Ford 42 Euro Const & Co Const Bdy

347

32 Sheepfold 637 Pile of Stones
BS Spr

Chapel Farm Blaenau Spr
Mon Fords Spr
317 Spr
The Capel-y-ffin 41 Waterfall
onastery Spr

Contours are given in metres
The vertical interval is 10m

A little way beyond the summit the view opens out and ahead you will see the trig point on Hay Bluff (Pen y Beacon), the end of the ridge on which you are walking. West is the Twmpa, the summit forming the end of the ridge across the Honddu Valley. A sharp descent of under 100 feet passes near a large rock outcrop, Llech y Lladron (the 'Robber's Stone') **43**, and reaches a junction of several paths. The one turning sharp east leads to the head of the Olchon Valley and the Cat's Back circuit route; to the north-east is the 'official' route of Offa's Dyke Path (see below); while the most obvious goes straight ahead towards Hay Bluff and is the one used by most Path walkers **C**. (The latter two routes together form an attractive half-day *circuit* – see map on page 73.)

The last path first: a further two-thirds of a mile (1 km) north-west over flat peat hags leads you to Hay Bluff (Pen y Beacon) **44** at 2,219 feet (677 metres) and your reward is a quite fantastic view north over Hay and the Wye Valley with the hills of south Radnorshire beyond: west are further Black Mountains edges and glimpses of the Brecon Beacons. Continue for a few yards to the northernmost point of the ridge and then turn sharp west down a clear path to a group of rocks **D**. Here turn north down a rhiw (gully) before swinging north-west over a common to the car park by the Gospel Pass road. You will have descended more than 600 feet (180 metres) in about half a mile. The road is busy with holiday traffic in summer, with sheep and ponies foraging for what the visitors will contribute, but it is unfenced and the verges are not unpleasant to walk on. This is just as well because you walk north-east by the road for more than half a mile (800 metres).

The indistinct official route swings north from the junction under Llech y Lladron and quite soon reaches the edge of the ridge with a sharp drop ahead and three gullies ('The Riggles') descending this. The Monnow rises here and the view over the low ridges eastwards is fine **45**. Turn north-west **E** along the ridge edge with the steep slopes of the top of Hay Bluff above you. Cross a col and now start to descend more quickly until the road is reached a little east of the straight descent described in the first option. Southbound walkers will have lovely views up to Hay Bluff after they begin the climb from the road.

Leave the road where a wall angles away from it and your route lies across the turf common about equidistant from the wall and the road **F**. You pass small old quarries on a rise and after a mile you reach the furthest corner of the common and go

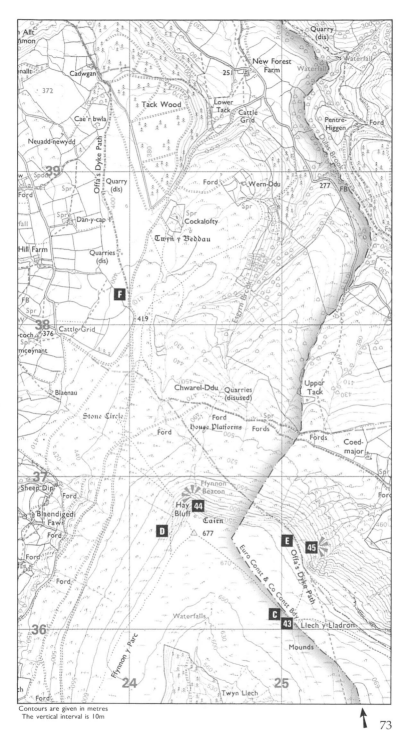

Contours are given in metres
The vertical interval is 10m

73

B4351 Clyro
1 km or ½ mile

Bricklands

Wyecliffe Cottages

HAY-ON-WYE (Y GELLI)

The Warren

53

Nant-y-glas-dwr Farm

Leam Lodge

Motte

Hay Castle

Sch

Llydyadyway

42

95   Cemy

HAY C

Offa's Dyke Path

Bryn Teg

Trewern

Cusop

46   Cusop Castle (site of)

Oakfield

Greenpit Farm

Clay Cottage

Brynmelin

Lower House

41

Caenantmelyn

Hay Common

Dyffryn

Water

Pen-y-common

Dan-y-fforest

Pant Barn

The Werns

Wernwilk House

Offa's Dyke Path

Wern Wood

Pant-y-fithel

22

23

Upper Danyforest

Tack Wood

24

Contours are given in metres
The vertical interval is 5m

through a gate north-west into a sunken lane.

Cross a stile north-east 350 yards beyond Cadwgan Farm. Descend two fields, admiring a sudden view of Hay and the Wye Valley, to a lane just east of upper Dan-y-fforest Farm (not Dan-y-fforest Farm, which is west of the Path). Cross a stone stile and continue descending a series of fields, soon beside a brook. The contrast with the moorlands you have just left is tremendous, though you are still losing height quickly. After a stretch of road north-west, cross further fields to follow the west side of the steep Cusop Dingle with the houses of this English outlier of Welsh Hay across the stream. A new route to avoid the road section here is currently (2000) planned, look out for waymarks. This is another magic place, with water-falls and corners full of spring flowers **46**. Suddenly Hay-on-

Wye is just in front of you and after a series of five kissing gates you reach the town by the car park, containing the Tourist Information Centre and toilets, with bus stops (to Hereford and Brecon) across the road. Hay is 2,000 feet (over 600 metres) below Hay Bluff, 5 miles (8 km) away.

The simplest way through the town is west from the car park and then north-east at a T-junction, past the clock tower, and north-west along the Clyro road and the bridge over the Wye. It is more interesting though to thread your way through the narrow streets circling the east side of the castle walls.

A CIRCULAR WALK FROM LLANTHONY ABBEY

8 miles (13 km) (see map on page 77)

While the majority of (inactive) visitors are content to admire Llanthony Abbey **40** (see page 82) from the valley road approach, the real glory of the ruins is only truly known to those who have surveyed it from above, on the Black Mountains ridge: the descent into the sylvan Vale of Ewyas from the ridge is a joyous and uplifting experience.

Park in the abbey car park (grid ref. 288 278). Retrace the approach road, going left (east) with the valley road. At the first bend leave the road left by the stile/gate to follow a tractor track south-east across a pasture to a stile/gate. The footpath follows the fence on the left, gently rising to reach a stile (crossing one of a succession of mountain streams on this traverse route to Cwmyoy). Keep alongside the left-hand hedge rising to another stile, and join the tractor track leading half left (notice tree-house on the right) down to a stile/gate. Follow the clear track via stiles/gates through Maes-y-Beran farmyard, going south on the rutted bridlelane, not the farm access road. Continue beyond the gate following the track, and switch sides of the hedge via a gate; keep beside the hedge left to a stile. Go south via a gate, then half right to a stile, then on to a stile/gate and ford **47** (notice attractive waterfall left).

Here it is practical to shorten the walk by going east uphill on a bridlepath swinging north, either to ascend to the pass with Rhiw Arw or contour towards Wiral for a swifter return to Llanthony Abbey (3 miles/5 km).

Pass down through the sad and dejected ruins of Weild Farm. Cross the ensuing pasture diagonally, half right, via a stream to a stile. Go along the river banktop fence to a stile, continue just beneath the shallow bank down to a rail stile. Traverse the meadow to the ford-footbridge (do not cross), and cross the stile on the left, taking the track up through the light woodland following the clearly waymarked path beside the hedge up to a stile. Rise half left up to a gate, on to a track up to a gate beside the outhouses of Daren-uchaf. Pass in front of the farmhouse to a gate, then follow the re-routed track left from the corrugated hut above Daren-ganol; keeping the fence to your right, contour the landslipped slopes to Daren-isaf, taking admiring glances left to the imposing crag of Cwmyoy Darren. The best view of Cwmyoy Darren is from the point where a track rises left. You can follow the bridleway, but the lower route allows you to visit St Martin's Church at Cwmyoy **48**. Pass through the yard, via gates, contouring the ensuing bank to a gate in an enclosure corner. Descend half right to enter a short lane at a stile/gate, and follow the road to enter the churchyard right.

Landslipping has not only created the splendid rock features of Cwmyoy Darren and Graig (grid ref. 300 237), but has also caused this sturdy church to tilt alarmingly. Miraculously, the buttresses have held in abeyance its long-threatened demise. Continue via the stony confined path rising from above the church ('way to hill' sign confirming the route, rather than the road to Penywern). Fork right, still within a narrow path, then follow the path with the wall on the right beneath the boulder-strewn craggy flanks of Graig, re-entering left a confined pathway to pass a lone cottage. Shortly after this, the bridlepath reaches a gate. Pass on down the muddy lane by the derelict Ty-hwnt-y-bwlch ('the house beyond the pass', the gap to the north of Graig). Follow the bridleway via gates, by a fence right, to a ford above Blanyoy, then turn half left up a rise to a gateway in the upper bounding wall. Ascend the steep mountain side, guided initially by a clear turf path, up through the heather and bog **G**, to the main ridgetop track, where you join Offa's Dyke Path to traverse Hatterrall Hill northwards.

The high, parallel Black Mountains ridges, culminating in Waun Fach (2,660 feet/810 metres), are in view to the north-west during the long gradual descent to the Llanthony/Longtown cross path. From the pass descend west on a clear shelf track, pass below a wooden memorial cross and ford small streams, the final one on the flat near the ruins of former farm buildings. Cross the stile, swing south-west over fields and through a wood; then make for the north end of the abbey ruins below you. The views over the whole descent are truly memorable **49**.

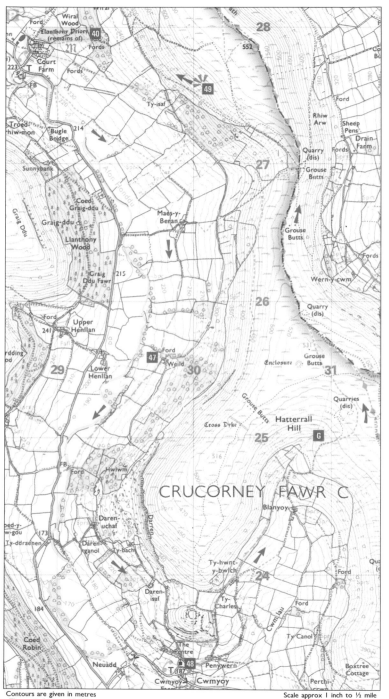

Contours are given in metres
The vertical interval is 10m

Scale approx 1 inch to ½ mile

The Vale of Ewyas with its small fields edged with broad-leaved trees.

A link route to Longtown and Olchon Valley Circuit (via Black Hill picnic site)
6 miles (9.7 km)

From the Llanthony/Longtown cross path (grid ref. 307 270) descend east with Rhiw Arw ('the mountain path of the pointed enclosure') passing above the two upper enclosures, then cross the contouring tractor track to go through a gate and enter a short descending lane.

At the bottom of the lane go left through the gate, veering left to follow the hedge downhill (one hedge removed) to a lightly fenced gateway. Continue through further gates, to pass through Cayo farmyard. Follow the farm road, descend to the footbridge over Olchon Brook, and then follow a metalled lane to ascend into Longtown **50** (see page 82), less than 2 miles (3 km) from Hatterrall Ridge.

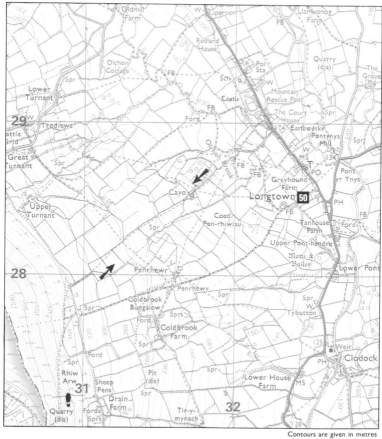

Contours are given in metres
The vertical interval is 10m

The view along the Cat's Back Ridge.

From Longtown the Path can of course be regained by retracing your route. Alternatively you can follow the little road for 2 miles (3.2 km) north to Llanveynoe **51** where there are Celtic crosses in the minute church of St Beuno. Continue along this road, eventually rejoining the Path approaching Hay Bluff, either via the Olchon Valley path or via the Cat's Back Ridge from the Black Hill picnic site 2 miles north-west of Llanveynoe (see page 85).

The Black Mountains

South of Hay, the northern edge of the Black Mountains forms a steep scarp where hard rocks overlie the softer Old Red Sandstone. From here, high ridges run south-eastward, with deep valleys between, sheltering magic, hidden places – Llanthony Abbey (see below) with Capel-y-ffin monastery, founded in 1870, further up the Honddu Valley; in the Olchon Valley to the east, the minute hamlet of Llanveynoe and the local metropolis of Longtown, with its castle of about 1300, a pub and *two* shops; eastwards again the fragmentary remains of Craswall Abbey.

The Path follows the longest of the ridges, the Hatterrall: often spectacular, usually windswept, and frequently boggy. It presents quite a different challenge from the detailed route-finding of the farmland to the south. The shorter ridge to the east, the Cat's Back, is a rocky knife edge, very exciting and recommended for a circular walk (see page 85). Further west, the ridges are higher but not so long or straight.

South-west of the Black Mountains, beyond the River Usk, lie the higher Brecon Beacons, which give their name to the national park that includes both these mountain areas.

Llanthony Abbey (or Priory) **40**

Under the care of Cadw, this is perhaps the most beautifully sited of the three monastic ruins near the Offa's Dyke Path, between the woods and fields of the Honddu Valley and the moorlands of the Hatterrall. It was founded in 1103, on the site of an earlier chapel dedicated to St David, by William de Lacy of the powerful Marcher family, who renounced the world and became a hermit there. Most of the surviving buildings were built by 1115, in the transitional Norman style: the nave of the church with two towers, part of the choir and transepts and the prior's lodging, now appropriately converted to the Abbey Hotel.

The monks were Augustinian canons, perhaps less tenacious than the Cistercians of Tintern and Valle Crucis, near Llangollen, for within a few years, deterred by Welsh raiders and the isolation of the place, many had left to found a new Llanthony in the more congenial surroundings of Gloucester. A few canons remained, and there were occasional revivals of prosperity, but the abbey was burnt by Owain Glyndwr and little was left by the time of the Dissolution in 1535. In 1807 the estate was bought by the poet Walter Savage Landor, who planted many of the fine trees still to be seen, but he too found life here intolerable and left in 1814.

Another revival came further up the valley in 1870, where the eccentric Father Ignatius (Rev. J. L. Lyne) founded a monastery, also called Llanthony, high above Capel-y-ffin **41** for Anglican Benedictines. This declined soon after his death in 1908: the ruins of this badly built church can also be visited. The house was bought by the artist Eric Gill in 1924 and he too established a community here (but this survived for only four years) and converted and decorated part of the buildings as a small chapel. For a short while it became a youth hostel and one of the authors

The 12th century ruins of Llanthony Abbey, set against the Honddu Valley.

Longtown Castle, crowned by one of the earliest circular keeps in Britain.

recalls spending an eerie New Year's Eve there (1949–50). You can see the buildings by courtesy of the owners.

In the hamlet of Capel-y-ffin there are two small churches, Anglican and Baptist, charming and simple buildings, and a little up the valley, and of importance to walkers, is the King George VI Memorial Youth Hostel.

A CIRCULAR WALK IN THE OLCHON VALLEY
$9\frac{1}{2}$ miles (15.5 km) (see maps on pages 86 and 87)

Walk from the Black Hill picnic site near Llanveynoe (grid ref. 287 327). Cross the stile and abruptly ascend the marked path (open *de facto* access) up the Cat's Back ridge, an apt description for this remarkably narrow rocky crest 52 H. Pass the large cairn, adjacent to signs of minor slate-quarrying, before the ridge broadens to the heather moor of Black Hill, named, as the Black Mountains themselves, from the dark profile they form when surveyed from the Herefordshire lowlands. Below, to the east, is the country so well described in Bruce Chatwin's evocative novel, *On the Black Hill*, and the film of the book includes some splendid photography of the area.

Passing the Ordnance Survey trig point and several shallow peaty pools, follow the edge path along Crib y Garth overlooking the Craswall Valley. Heading north-west, join the path from the Olchon Valley, which may conveniently be used as a short-cut return for a walk of 5 miles (8 km), then drift left to join Offa's Dyke Path beneath the Llech y Lladron rock 43.

Walk south along the broad peat path on top of the Black Mountains ridge for 3 miles (5 km) (which can be toilsome if the peat is at all wet B), *en route* traversing two tops to reach a cairn and stake at the Capel-y-ffin/Olchon cross path. Go left, north-east; the 'rhiw' path becomes evident slanting left, then right where a shepherd's path joins from the edge of the moor (some walkers may prefer to follow the exhilarating thin sheep trod along the edge from the head of the Olchon Valley, linking up at this point). Shortly after, branch left to descend the funnelling of the enclosures, on the footpath leading via two gates directly on to the valley road. Go left, along the road sweeping round Blaen Olchon to join, left, the ascending approach road to the picnic site.

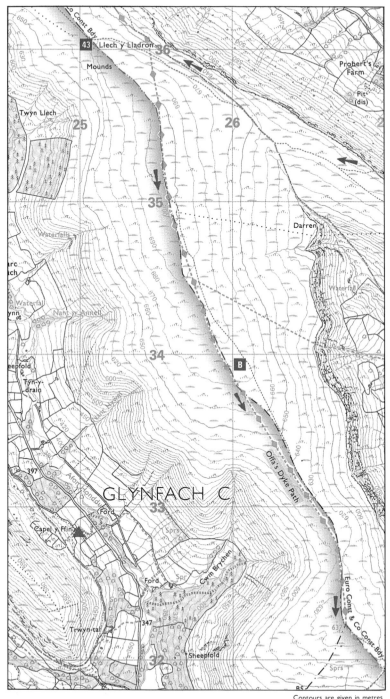

Contours are given in metres
The vertical interval is 10m

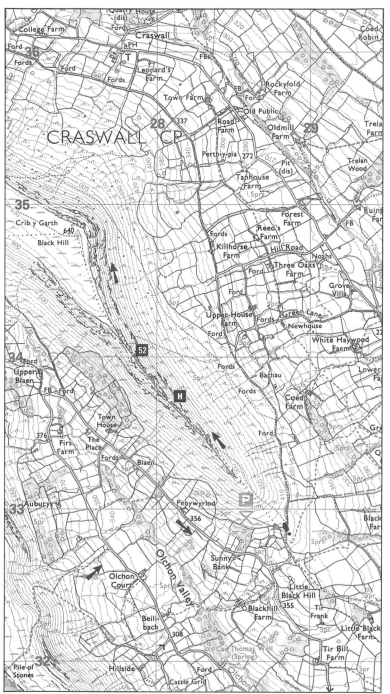

Contours are given in metres
The vertical interval is 10m

Longtown 50

Originally 'the borough of Ewyas Lacy', Longtown was the centre of the de Lacy territory. The castle is at the top end of a spur overlooking the River Monnow. The main feature is the motte, crowned by one of the earliest circular keeps in Britain (late 12th or early 13th century). The inner and outer baileys are separated by a wall with a gateway flanked by two turrets.

Hay-on-Wye 53

For the last 20 years Hay has been famous as the 'capital' of the second-hand book trade, an activity started by Richard Booth and now ranging from shops with jumbled stacks from which you can buy very cheaply indeed, if you can find what you want, to those selling valuable antiquarian books or specialising in particular subjects. If you are interested in books you need to allow several hours for browsing, but walkers must remember how heavy books are. There are regular special buses from London to 'the bookshops of Hay'! With the books have come people interested in literature and the arts: a week-long literary festival, started in 1988, takes place in May.

The name 'Hay' comes from the same Old English word as 'hedge' and there are other references to a defensive, hedged enclosure, but the exact site of this is not known. The town originally seems to have been built in two stages: first St Mary's Church, founded about 1120 (but nothing of the original survives) and a castle mound of about the same date, to the west; then, across a dingle to the east, the later castle and planned borough. The square keep of the castle was built about 1200 but has many later additions; the adjoining house dates from 1660, but has recently been damaged by fire. Stone walls round this part of the town were built in 1237 but only fragments remain near the market area and off Newport Street. The town was the scene of many incidents in the struggles between the English and Welsh in the 13th century. The centre of the town is an attractive maze of narrow streets with buildings of all periods, including the Butter and Cheese Markets of the 1830s, leading down to the clock tower of 1881 so typical of many mid-Wales towns.

Hay has featured in recent films, including *On the Black Hill*, based on the Bruce Chatwin novel, and *Dandelion Dead*, Michael Chaplin's ITV filming of the infamous, but true, Armstrong murder case.

Evening strolls from Hay-on-Wye

Walkers seeking an evening stroll from Hay have a choice of riverside paths on the town side of the Wye Bridge. *Either* follow the Bailey footpath south-west from the town side of the bridge: this route continues down beneath the modern bridge and along the wooded river bank (not with the old railway track-bed), diverting left to an anglers' car park on The Warren from the northern tip of the Wye bend, and then backtracking. *Alternatively*, follow part of the Wye Valley walk north-east from the bridge, again backtracking.

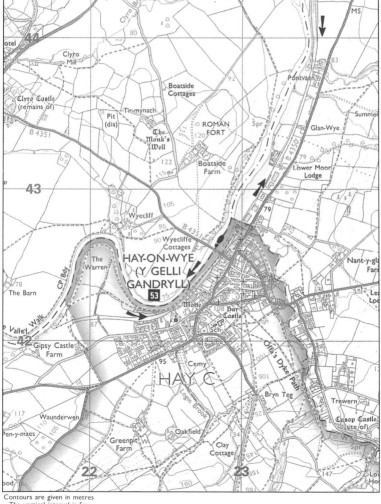

Contours are given in metres
The vertical interval is 5m

Hay in winter, seen across the River Wye.

4 Hay to Kington

through Newchurch and Gladestry
14¾ miles (23.3 km)

This section makes a very pleasant day's walk, in Wales, rising from the Wye Valley into the hills of Radnorshire, yet never far from the border with Herefordshire. Fragmentary remains of Offa's Dyke are well to the east, though coming closer to you all the time! In the southern part of the section you are in 'Kilvert Country' (see page 102). Further north the moorland ridges of Disgwylfa and Hergest are dominant. This is where the only regular sporting event on the Path is held, the annual 'Offa's Dyke 15', a Hay-to-Kington charity cross-country race.

Leave Hay by the Clyro road, noting below you, before the bridge over the Wye, the track of the former Hereford to Hay railway, now a riverside walk; there is also a picnic site by the bridge. From the bridge **54** the Wye makes a fine scene with its overhanging trees and you may well see fishing both by humans and birds, such as herons. Turn north-east off the road immediately after the bridge, down some steps and then go straight on through the wood above the river. This is a favourite stretch for family walks by local people. After a while you emerge on to and then follow a quiet stretch of the river bank **55**. At the top of the field above there are the square corners of a 'Gaer', a temporary marching camp built by the Romans during their drive up the Wye Valley **56**. Three-quarters of a mile (1 km) beyond the bridge you veer away from the river and cross a field to reach a cultivated area. Your way for the next mile or so is by well-waymarked field edges and tracks.

Cross a plank footbridge two fields beyond a large new barn and slope up to the A438 – the busy Brecon to Hereford road. Take great care in crossing it, and in the 300 yards you walk on it north-eastwards: there are wide verges, and you *must* enjoy the quite superb view of the Wye from here **57**. Just beneath you is a bend with a spectacular view along the river in each direction: east with a distant prospect of the ruins of the 13th century Clifford Castle and south to Hay with Hay Bluff rising beyond.

The little lane you follow off the main road soon divides and here you cross a stile between the forks to go up the south side of Bettws Dingle. Below are steeply wooded slopes as you follow an enclosed path at the bottom edge of two long fields, crossing a stile partway along to walk in the wood. Two fine barns up

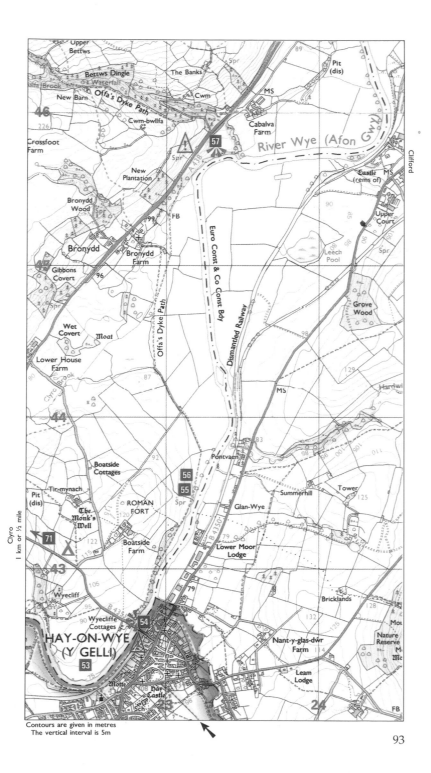

Contours are given in metres
The vertical interval is 5m

93

the hill to the left are now, alas, falling into decay. Then, through a gateway, descend the track, usually muddy, into the dingle. You cross quite high above the stream on an earth bridge. Rise steeply and soon swing west through a gloomy patch of firs to emerge into the daylight, up some steps and on to a minor road.

The next mile or so is road work, first north and then, after a junction, east towards Rhydspence, where the inn on the A438 over a mile from the Path is a noted half-timbered building. Just past the junction a turning south-east, off the Path, leads across a field to Bettws Chapel **58**, one of the churches where Francis Kilvert preached, walking more than 3 miles from Clyro in all weathers. It is a simple building, largely rebuilt in 1878 but with good surviving medieval woodwork in the roof and screen.

Back on the Path, soon you leave the road to go north up the middle of two fields, then back to the road again at Cae Higgin Farm. Continue north and uphill for another quarter of a mile, swing north-west, then climb northwards up a muddy green lane. On the hedgerow trees there are fine examples of witches' broom. Over a small summit, with superb views south, **59**, you reach a T-junction. Take the road straight ahead. After one-third of a mile (530 metres) you swing west, cross a stile, and swing north again, east of a grazing area. After more than $2\frac{1}{2}$ miles (4 km) on minor roads, you are returning to real paths.

The short east–west stretch of lane you have just left is Roman in origin and leads, westwards, to a square, unexplained enclosure (marked 'camp' on the map) on the top of Little Mountain just west of the Path **60**; the Roman route can be traced eastwards towards their major settlement at Magnis, west of Hereford. Over the summit of the Little Mountain ridge (at 1,100 feet/350 metres) a new prospect suddenly opens up **61**. The village of Newchurch is below, and Radnor Forest is prominent on the horizon ahead. Descend through gorse and foxgloves towards Gilfach-yr-heol Farm, then swing sharply east of it to join a road. This crosses the Cwmila Brook before taking you into Newchurch.

The few cottages are grouped near the church, mainly rebuilt in 1856, but containing a font which may be pre-Norman. South of the church is the well-restored Great House **62**, a timber-framed building with the widest domestic cruck in Wales (1490). This was an early form of timber framing, consisting of pairs of great curved timbers placed vertically to support the walls and then meeting at the top to support the roof.

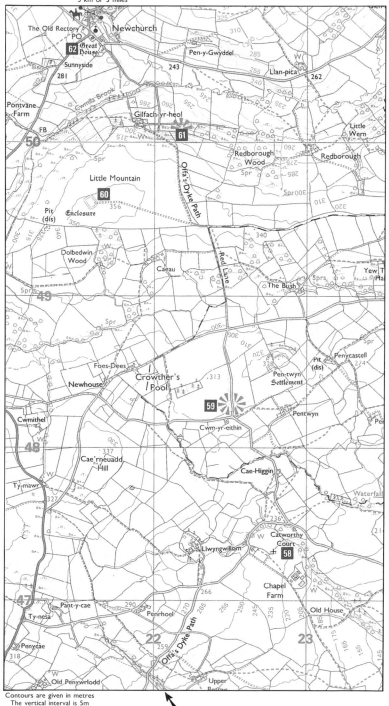

B4594 Gladestry
5 km or 3 miles

Contours are given in metres
The vertical interval is 5m

95

Go through the hamlet on the Gladestry road and, just over the bridge, turn east through a neat farmyard. An enclosed lane soon swings north-east on to Disgwylfa Hill 63, a pocket-size version of the open moorland of Hergest a little further north. You climb directly ahead, first with a fence to the east, and then follow a line of concrete posts, just frequent enough to ensure your route: this is good waymarking. The short turf is pleasant to the feet and the climb is fairly gentle. There are two rises and two falls in 1½ miles (about 2.5 km) with a pond in the first dip: moorland ponies are usually to be seen nearby.

After the second descent you must take care to turn sharply north-west towards Hill House Farm: a friendly place with a neat yard and a water tap 64 with a verse welcoming the walker – 'It's cool, it's fresh, it's free', etc. Leave via the drive of the farm, turn east along a road, and in a few yards a stile shows you the route continuing northwards: at first by a wood, and then down the middle of a long field aiming for the end of the east side of the hedge of the next field. This is cultivated farmland and it is all too easy to go adrift A. You should reach a small road with a large new house, built on the footings of an attractive old barn, a little way ahead.

The Path has been realigned to avoid this house, Fairfields (formerly Stonehouse Barn). Turn east on the road, and soon after this cross a stile to resume the northward walk between two fences. Then climb to the top corner B of this first field, over a stile and along the headland of the next field to the stile by the two gates.

Then go down a wide, new farm track: look carefully for signs directing you off this eastwards towards the west, top, side of a gully C, parallel to the farm track. The gully is then crossed and a series of stiles and gates lead you to the road to the east of Stonehouse Farm. From here it is an easy half-mile (800 metres) north-west into Gladestry. During all the complex navigation south of Stonehouse you should still have noted the striking view 65 of Hergest Ridge ahead as you came over the last ridge.

You pass the Vale of Arrow football club and join the B4594 just before it crosses Gladestry Brook, a tributary of the Arrow. Swing east along Gladestry village street 66 (see page 106). Beyond the Royal Oak continue on a minor road where the main one swings north. In about 200 yards fork steeply up a narrow lane past further houses and soon you emerge on to the open moorland turf of Hergest Ridge 67.

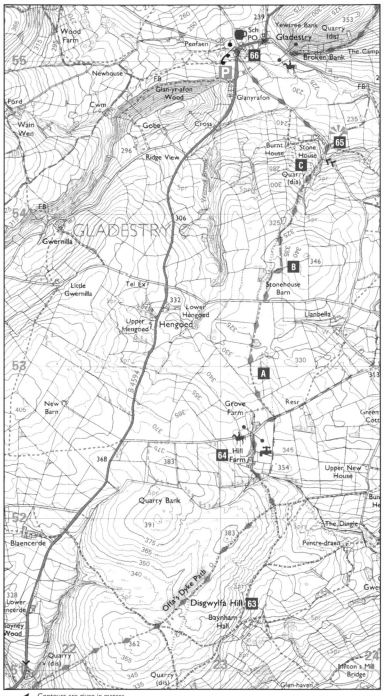

Contours are given in metres
The vertical interval is 5m

Take the principal path ahead, not the lower one by the hedge. Soon, at a col, take the middle one of three uphill routes with occasional posts marking the Path. (If walking the Path north–south, when coming off the ridge at this point swing down to the enclosed lane rather than continuing ahead to an isolated summit.) This moorland section is nearly 3 miles (5 km) long and once on the long west-to-east ridge you simply follow it at over 1,300 feet (400 metres), enjoying the firm surface, probably a breeze, and extensive views northwards **68**; mostly you are just north of the actual top and so the southern view is limited. Hanter Hill and Worsell Wood are the nearer summits

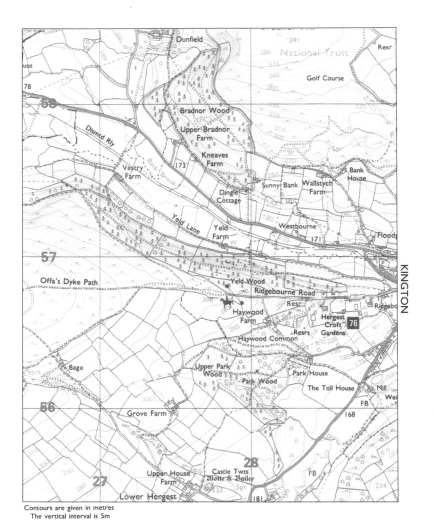

Contours are given in metres
The vertical interval is 5m

and further off are Radnor Forest and, to the east, the ranges beyond Kington that you will soon reach.

Horses roam this ridge, often seen drinking at the two ponds you pass, and you may encounter riders since Gladestry to Kington is the longest of the few bridleways on our Path. Gorse provides striking colour and wild thyme is also in evidence.

Near the middle of the ridge you will cross the site of the former Kington racecourse **69**, the curving tracks still quite clear. The Whet Stone **70**, a large glacial boulder, is a landmark just north of the Path at this point. For the rest of your route into Kington, see page 108.

The Wye and Hay Bluff, a distinctive feature as seen from the north.

A CIRCULAR WALK TO CLYRO

3½ miles (5.6 km)

From Hay, cross the Wye bridge, continuing up the B4351 to the road on the right, at the entrance to Radnors End camping ground. Follow the left-hand hedge, passing through the gate and over the succeeding two stiles. Then advance through a series of gates: after reaching the first one proceed north-west to a second gate, then north-north-west to a third gate in the corner of the field. With Clyro **71** in your sights descend the elongated field to a stile, continue towards Clyro Church via a gate in a single-strand fence, passing the sewage works to a gate. Cross the A438. Follow the short path between Clyro Post Office and Ashbrook House, home from 1865–72 of the famous Victorian diarist, Rev. Francis Kilvert (see below). Continue right, past the Baskerville Arms Hotel, then fork left up the road signposted 'Newchurch 5½'. Ascend, initially steeply, passing the splendidly sited Sundew Cottage, from where walkers can enjoy the lush sweep of the Wye Valley, dominated by the Black Mountains scarp, with Hay Bluff prominent. Turn right down the lane at Court Evan Gwynne, descending in intimate surroundings on a bedrock path to the A438. Go left, then right along the byway leading past Tir-mynach Farm ('the monk's land', once associated with Abbey Cwmhir) to Radnors End.

Clyro **71**

This picturesque village off the A438 has been much extended by modern housing. It is best known because of the curacy, from 1865 to 1872, of Francis Kilvert, some of whose diaries were discovered and published in the late 1930s. His accounts of the countryside and its people in his time are an important social document as well as delightful reading. Serious Border walkers should make a special point of reading at least the abridged paperback version of the diaries (see page 142), to savour something of this perceptive commentator on rural life. Kilvert was a great walker, thinking nothing of walking the ten hilly miles to Capel-y-ffin to visit Father Ignatius at his monastery and then walking back the same day. Television programmes have contributed greatly to the fame of his work – and of Clyro.

Apart from the tower, which is older, St Michael's Church where Kilvert ministered dates from 1853. He lived at Ashbrook

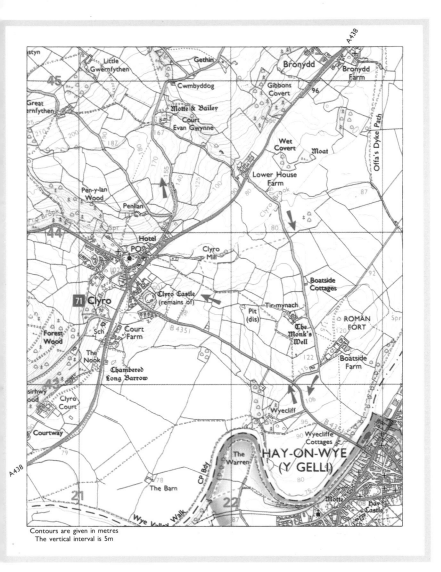

Contours are given in metres
The vertical interval is 5m

House, a pleasant stone building dating from the early 19th century, which has a commemorative plaque put up by the Kilvert Society. It is now an art gallery where you can also buy cards and books of local and Kilvert interest. Opposite is the Baskerville Arms, with a large stone dog sitting above the porch – it was here, at Clyro Court, south-west of the village, that Sir Arthur Conan Doyle wrote his classic Sherlock Holmes detective story, *The Hound of the Baskervilles*. This is believed to be based on the local countryside, though nominally set in south-west England. A trail guide to Clyro is available at the church.

A CIRCULAR WALK ON HERGEST RIDGE
5 miles (8 km)

Park on the verge near the old railway building off the A44 at Stanner (grid ref. 261 583). Leave the B4594 Gladestry road (now re-routed on to the trackbed of the old New Radnor railway) on a footpath signposted left through a wicket gate. Cross the meadow, on a track, to a footbridge and ford. Pass through a gate to follow the forestry track, right, below Worsell Wood, keeping beside the hedge to pass beyond Lower Hanter Farm via three gates. Branch sharp left at the standpipe, off the road to Rock Cottage. Ascend the path on to a track passing Middle Hanter Cottage, through a hedged lane. The track continues past rustic caravans, where walkers with the energy can add the mountain-like summit of Hanter Hill (1,358 feet/414 metres) **72** to their itinerary: branch from the ascending track right, up the rocky east ridge **D**, traverse the summit (no cairn), and descend on the clear path leading south-east to the col. On the main walk, at the fork, keep on the higher path leading to a signpost on the col, which is the frontier between England and Wales.

Continuing (into England) take the track slanting east up on to Hergest Ridge **67**. Cross over the old racecourse, passing the Whet Stone in the gorse to join Offa's Dyke Path. Maintaining an eastward descending line, cross the racecourse again, and after ¾ mile (1 km) branch from the Path where a clear track leads obliquely left through the bracken opposite a gate in the enclosure on the right. The green track declines, following the top side of the conifer plantation, then descends more steeply to a forestry track. Cross the facing stile to follow a farm track across Birchen Coppice and left into the pasture **E**. Contour westward via the field gate left of the holly tree: this old hedge is the England–Wales border. Reaching a stream (which enters the old orchard), cross the fence in the corner and, ignoring waymark left, turn sharp right to the gate. Take care underfoot when crossing the wayward flowing stream, and in the muddy farmyard beyond. Pass with care through the farm building going left of the red brick farmhouse to a fence stile. OS maps differ in their spelling of this farm, Rowbatch being the incorrect English form, Rhiw-fach ('the small mountain path') the correct Welsh form **73**. Contour the pasture on an indistinct track to cross into the foot of Worsell Wood above Gilwern Brook. Follow the forestry track which rises, then descends, to the gate and the footbridge over the brook.

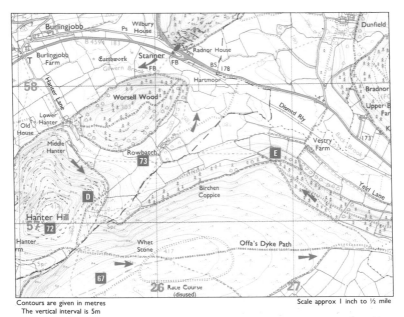

Contours are given in metres
The vertical interval is 5m

Scale approx 1 inch to ½ mile

The south-west end of Hergest Ridge, with bracken fronds emerging.

Sunlit gravestones in St Mary's Churchyard, Gladestry.

Gladestry 66

This is more of a 'real' village than most of those you pass through on Offa's Dyke Path, with a shop, the Royal Oak public house, a weekly bus and a neat school serving a wide area.

St Mary's Church is large and attractive with features dating from four centuries. The nave is 13th century with a good 15th century roof, the chancel 14th century with roof and windows 200 years newer. Old stone houses in the village street complete the composition. Gladestry Brook is a tributary of the River Arrow.

Hergest Court 74

A mile south-east of the Ridge, this is the 15th century remnant of a greater house. Although in Herefordshire, in its heyday this was a centre of Welsh culture, and here was preserved 'The Red Book of Hergest', now in Oxford, from which derives the collection of legends, many featuring King Arthur and his Knights, known as *The Mabinogion*.

Kington Camp 75

A little further south are the remains of Kington Camp which, during the last war, was one of the largest American military hospitals in Britain. The few sad huts, some used as factories, cannot convey the scene as it was in the 1940s.

5 Kington to Knighton

via Dolley Green
13½ miles (21.7 km)

This stretch is, in our highly prejudiced eyes, the most enjoyable day's walk of the whole Path. You are back with the Dyke as your constant companion, the route is hilly but not unduly steep, and the views are superb – both distant and close to. In short, the essence of this Path, in traversing an unspoilt borderland, is to be found here.

The route eastwards off Hergest Ridge into Kington Town is on a narrow descending lane. Before Kington is Hergest Croft **76**, with gardens containing show collections of rhododendrons, azaleas and many exotic trees. It is open to the public from May to October and there is a car park by the lane.

The tower of St Mary's Church, seen directly ahead from the Hergest lane, welcomes the walker to the town. The best route through is by the south side of the churchyard and through the lych gate down Church Road. Turn into The Square by The Swan, go round to the top furthest corner, then down by the old National School to descend Crooked Well to the river. Most walkers will wish to explore and use the facilities of the town and for this you continue down past The Swan to the Market Hall and High Street.

The bottom of Crooked Well is pretty, with old cottages and resident ducks. The footbridge over Back Brook, a tributary of the Arrow, leads immediately to the A44, the busy Kington bypass, so take the utmost care. You climb the steep lane opposite but soon branch off up the centre of a paddock and get increasingly breathless as you climb to Kington golf course by a path between neat cottages. They, and you, have a fine view south to the town and the Black Mountains beyond **78**.

The golf course, on National Trust land on Bradnor Hill **79**, is the highest in England, rising to 1,284 feet (390 metres), and must be one of the most pleasantly situated of any. You cross a corner of it (yes, the golfers do call 'Fore' to walkers in the way), keeping just west of the cottages ahead at the point where you emerge on Bradnor Green. A little sharp navigation, and a close watch on the stiles, is now needed **A**. First take a short enclosed track directly away (north-east) from the golf course, then aim for the furthest visible corner of a wood, keeping well above a new bungalow. Continue to walk in a northerly direction across

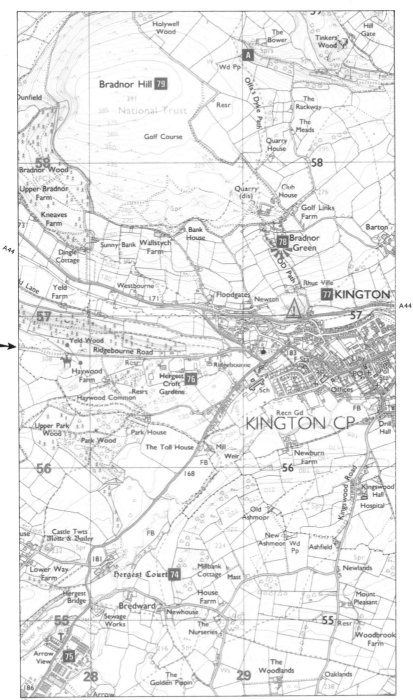

Contours are given in metres
The vertical interval is 5m

109

Contours are given in metres
The vertical interval is 5m

three more fields to reach a corner of a larch wood in a hollow coming up from the east. Continue above the wood to the next stile and then swing north-east and climb towards the ridge of Rushock Hill seen ahead of you.

The chief feature here is your return to Offa's Dyke **80** after 54 miles (87 km). It runs on the ridge of the hill and you reach it at a gap which may have been a traffic control gateway. A short way to the east are three yews, the Three Shepherds **81**. These were planted in the 18th century by the Garbett sisters from nearby Knill Court and are a landmark for many miles. The predecessor of the eastern yew died some years ago but a subscription raised by Offa's Dyke Association walkers led to its quick replacement. The new tree seems to be doing well but it will be '2½' Shepherds for many years yet. The Dyke does continue south-east, but it is only fragmentary in its course to the Wye west of Hereford.

Turn west by the Dyke: you are now more than 1,200 feet (360 metres) high and Hergest, and the East Radnor hills you are approaching, provide the mid-distance views. You soon reach a 'corner' of the Dyke and Path where the route follows the high ground south-west **82**, thus maintaining its dominance over 'Wales'. A col between Rushock and Herrock Hills is the next landmark **83**. You have dropped a little but there is a new view west to the hills south-west of Radnor Forest.

The Dyke here continues on to Herrock, circling it a little under the top; the Path, however, turns abruptly north and drops down from the col along the east side of the hill. Take care here to keep quite high on the slope at first as there are other paths dropping from the col that go too far east **B**. The view below soon opens out **84**: Hindwell Valley and Knill Court below with Burfa Hill and its hill fort ahead. Swing west near the bottom of the slope, with Herrock now to the south. Pass below a cottage and soon you go through a wicket gate to circle a field and reach the B4362 by the extensive Lower Harpton Farm.

Walk one-third of a mile (530 metres) north-east along the busy, winding B road. On reaching the 17th century bridge, listed as 'of historic interest' **85** (from late 1994 vehicles will be on a new parallel bridge), look south at Herrock and the clear line of Dyke descending towards you **86**. Turn north-west by the cottage over the bridge and soon fork on a forestry road up the side of Burfa Hill. A little way up this, take care to take the left, level fork through a belt of woodland on a green track.

The restored medieval farmhouse at Burfa, on the Path.

Pass Old Burfa **87** (see page 124), then a newer house and, after crossing the lane beyond, climb on to the Dyke and follow it along Barland Bank. A good route has been cleared so that walkers do not erode the Dyke by walking on its slopes. Note how the stream accentuates the depth of the ditch. The westward panorama across the Radnor Valley is at its best here **88**. Cross the Evenjobb to Presteigne road, staying on the west side of the Dyke, and soon you climb a flight of wooden steps to the top of the Dyke bank **89**. Beyond a forestry road contour through Granner Wood with steep slopes down to the west and circle the head of a cwm.

Beyond the cwm climb steeply to the top of the mixed woodland of Hilltop Plantation and then walk downhill to the Beggar's Bush road, passing just east of Pen Offa Farm. Just south of the road there is a gap in the Dyke, with inturned banks, indicating a probable traffic control point; it looks quite different from the usual crude farming cut-through **90**. The name Bwlch, a 'pass', just east, strengthens this hypothesis.

Ahead is the long descent to the Lugg Valley. Cross two fields, keeping east of the fence. This is a favourite stretch for walkers and photographers in all seasons, with superb views to the bottom and to Furrow Hill beyond, on the Dyke and punctuated by sturdy oaks **91**. Southbound walkers should take the climb gently and turn to admire the view north. From the road by Yew Tree Farm the Path leaves the line of the Dyke on a level route diagonally north-east beside a deep ditch to reach the bridge over the River Lugg, the home of otters and at least one pair of dippers. Look out for this black bird with its white 'bib' dipping and bobbing on rocks and branches in the river.

Follow the river for a few yards and then cross the bridge. The south-east edge of a large field leads to the B4356 at Dolley Green. Continue east on the road for 200 yards to the chapel and swing sharply north-west up a wide track. In spring this is truly a primrose path. At a small wood turn north, climbing all the time, along one of the new agricultural roads funded by Common Market grants. There is a fine view back across the Lugg Valley to the Dyke you have just descended, the Rushock yews and Hergest Ridge. Eventually a gully brings you back to the line of the much eroded Dyke on Furrow Hill **92**: follow it until it swings slightly east before an old Dutch barn on the horizon. There has been an exceptional view west since you rejoined the Dyke with Pilleth and its wellingtonias prominent (see circular walk on page 120).

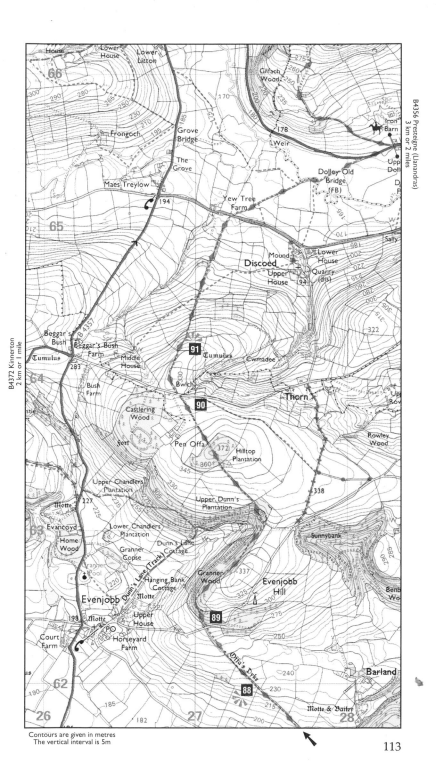

Contours are given in metres
The vertical interval is 5m

B4356 Presteigne (Llanandras)
3 km or 2 miles

B4372 Kinnerton
2 km or 1 mile

The route has been a bridleway since Dolley Green but, just before the Dutch barn, riders must go off east or west. The walker turns east by the barn, keeping to the south of the fence, skirts a dew pond and, after one field, turns north again having rejoined the Dyke. On a clear day, the view here ranges from the Malverns in the south-east to the Brecon Beacons in the south-west, over 30 miles in each direction **93**. The town of Presteigne is clear much nearer to the south-east. This is from a height of only 1,200 feet (360 metres). Go north from here, over the top of Hawthorn Hill, on a prominent but eroded section of Dyke between a series of fields. Beware of ant and mole hills and ankle-turning old rabbit warrens **C**; the rabbits provide the staple diet of buzzards, which are common in this area.

The Path passes down the west side of a small pine wood to reach a field containing an obelisk **94** to Sir Richard Green Price, who brought railways to Radnorshire. He was the local MP and lived nearby at Norton (to the south-east). Pass round a muddy pond and by a gorse patch to reach the B4355, the Knighton to Presteigne road. On the north side is a 19th century stone **95**, inscribed 'Offa's Dyke, made in the year AD 757' – but this was the *first* year of his reign. Cross the road at the layby and follow the Dyke over four fields to rejoin the B4355.

Looking north down Offa's Dyke to the fields of the Lugg Valley.

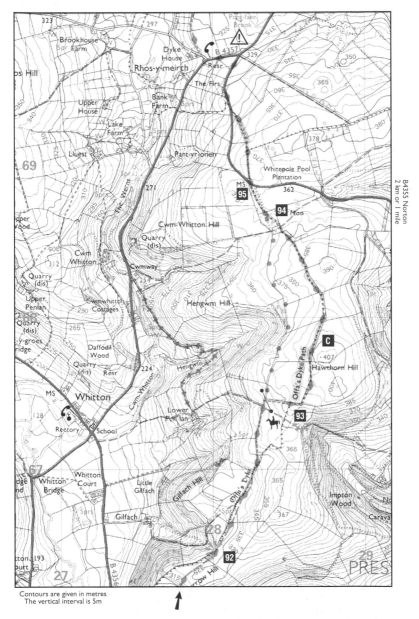

Contours are given in metres
The vertical interval is 5m

Continue north on the road for 350 yards, then take the B4357
turn at Rhôs-y-meirch for a further 200 yards. After a phone box,
take a little road turning off on the north side. Immediately go
over a stile to resume the Dykeside walk north. After four fields
you are on the west side of a massive stretch of the earthwork as

it falls then rises on either side of the Jenkin Allis traffic gap **96**, which has the most obvious of the inturned guard banks, or rather, had, until too-close ploughing did them no good. However, the Dyke marching north up the hill here gives as good an idea as any of what it was like and how steep were the gradients it took in its course.

Further towards Knighton, you cross to the east side of more eroded Dyke, soon with the town golf course to the east. The hills in the distance to the east are Titterstone Clee and Brown Clee, well to the east of Ludlow.

The steep descent now begins and Frŷdd Wood **97** lies ahead: you and the Dyke scramble steeply down its slopes to the garages situated behind the houses on Frŷdd Road. Turn east on the road, and immediately north again down steep Larkey Lane; cross the Knighton Hotel car park and then go through the arch ahead into Broad Street. You are now in Knighton **103**, 'the town on the Dyke', and almost halfway on the route going north. For your route through Knighton, see page 124.

The Offa's Dyke Park in Knighton, looking north towards Panpunton Hill.

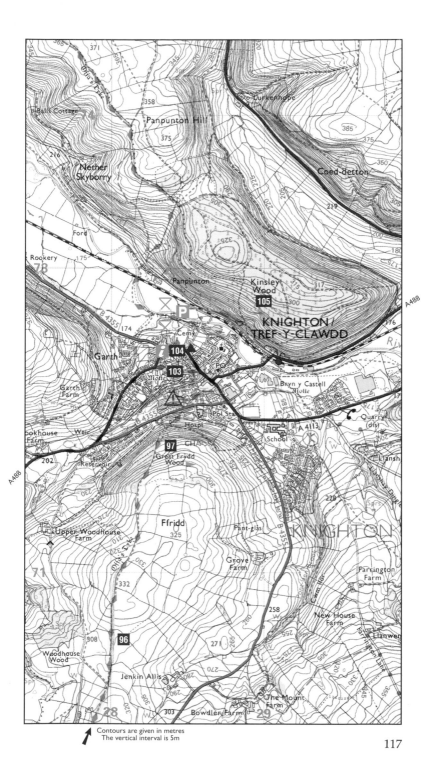

Contours are given in metres
The vertical interval is 5m

117

A CIRCULAR WALK FROM KINGTON
4 miles (6.4 km)

Park your car in The Square in Kington. Commence the walk
from here, leaving The Square at the top right-hand corner.
Follow Offa's Dyke Path (see page 108) across the Back Brook
Valley, over the bypass (A44) with great care, up to Bradnor
Green, on to Bradnor Hill **79** (National Trust property) and up
over the golf course (first and eighteenth fairways) to reach an
unenclosed road. Here turn left (north-west) from the Path
along that road, continuing until the point where the metalling
ends at a gate just after crossing a fairway. Turn left and follow
the fence for about 400 yards (0.5 km), admiring the view to the
north of Rushock Hill with Offa's Dyke and Herrock Hill.
Beyond a tee, contour left, first west then south to reach the
ninth tee. At this point **98**, there is a seat affording a wonderful
prospect, westward over Stanner to the Radnor Forest, swinging round over the hills behind Gladestry to Hanter Hill and
Hergest Ridge in the south-west.

Continue using sheep tracks due south, then turn half-left
down to the edge of Bradnor Wood. A sunken track leads, left,
round and down on to a track passing Walstych Farm, where a
metalled lane leads down into the Back Brook Valley. Cross over
the A44 bypass and follow Church Road back into Kington.

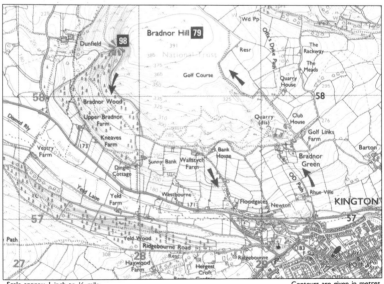

Scale approx 1 inch to ½ mile

Contours are given in metres
The vertical interval is 5m

Herrock Hill, with Offa's Dyke on a shelf near the top.

Kington 77

Kington, situated in Herefordshire but as Welsh as its neighbour Border towns, is another ancient borough established in two stages. You come down from Hergest into the oldest part of the town, with St Mary's Church on a high point and the castle behind it beside the Back Brook. The church tower and chancel date from the early 13th century; the nave was rebuilt about 1300 – the whole is well worth a visit. The castle can never have been a major building and only the high, overgrown mound remains, with no public access. The best way to see this is by following the streamside path westwards from the bottom of Crooked Well before you cross the river on your way north on the Path.

The main part of the town, referred to as 'New Kington' as early as 1267, is on the low ground east of the church where parallel lanes and long back gardens may preserve the pattern of the strips in the former open fields. Behind the red brick Victorian Market Hall, which incorporates the clock tower without which no Border town would be complete, is the museum, fronting a small paved square (named after its twin town in France, Marines).

A CIRCULAR WALK FROM RHÔS-Y-MEIRCH
6 miles (9.6 km)

Park on the verge near the telephone box at Rhôs-y-meirch (grid ref. 280 697). Walk north-west along the minor road beyond Dyke House, turning first left (south) on the road opposite a holly tree, then west along the farm lane to Radnor House. Continue past the farmhouse along the lane and subsequent track via a series of gates crossing Rhôs Hill. The track descends into Cwm-blewyn, sweeping round by the farm on to the gated access road (south-east). Emerging from the side valley the views ahead **99** are of the northern foothills of Radnor Forest, and in the Lugg Valley notice the considerable motte and bailey earthworks of Castell Foel-allt. Approaching Pilleth Court Farm, St Mary's Church **100** is prominent on the facing hillside (see page 124). Reach the B4356 via gates through the farmyard. Divert right to join the track to the church. In spring the terraced churchyard bears an abundance of daffodils.

Returning to the entrance to Pilleth Court, turn left. Either follow the road directly to Whitton or, more attractively, after a few yards go through the first gate right down the track passing Castell Foel-allt **101** to a bridge over the River Lugg. Beyond the river ascend to join the Litton track, advancing left via gates to Bridge End Farm, then turn left along the road to Whitton crossroads.

Walk south along the Presteigne road, turning left through the gate immediately after the Cwm Whitton Brook Bridge. Follow the stream on the rutted track up to a fragile gate. Climb directly uphill (note: hedge removed) to the staggered hedgeline **D**. Cross the netting fence, continue alongside the new fence on the right, switching sides at the gate, and climb to a stile into the fence corner below Lower Pen-lan. Slant up right, passing through the old farmyard and left on the approach track. Immediately after the farm gate turn sharp right, rising with the surfaced track beside the hedge **E**. On reaching a gate conclude the ascent up the open pasture to an old Dutch barn on Hawthorn Hill, where you join Offa's Dyke Path, going left to Rhôs-y-meirch.

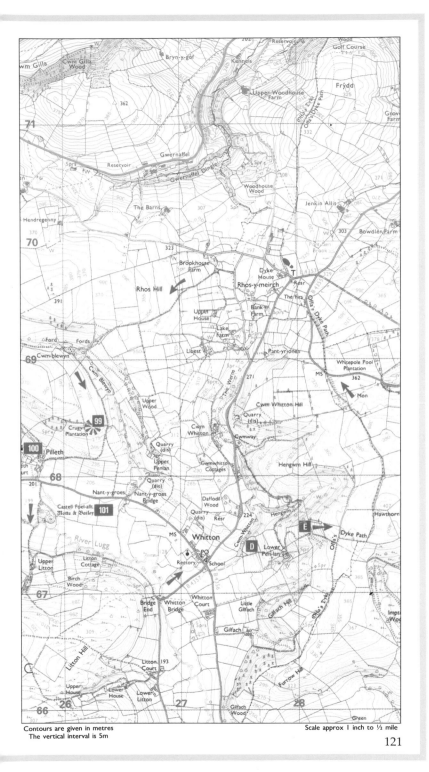

Contours are given in metres
The vertical interval is 5m

Scale approx 1 inch to ½ mile

121

A winter evening view towards Black Mixen and Radnor Forest.

Old Burfa 87

The fine timber-framed house was a complete ruin as recently as the 1960s, but was lovingly restored by the local architect Michael Garner. The earliest part, nearest the Path, is over 600 years old, and much of the rest is early 17th century Jacobean with painting on the internal woodwork.

Burfa Hill is above to the south-east. It is crowned by a fine Iron Age hill fort with several high banks and ditches, partly concealed by forestry. It is not clear whether Offa's Dyke climbed the hill to use these banks or skirted the lower slopes.

Presteigne (Llanandras)

Just over two miles (3 km) east of the Path at Dolley Green, Presteigne is a pretty town in the sheltered Lugg Valley. St Andrew's Church, in a large secluded churchyard, has traces of its Saxon origin and much work from the 14th and 15th centuries: it is frequently used for concerts. This was once the county and assize town for Radnorshire and the classical Shire Hall of 1829, in the well-named Broad Street, is now a fascinating local museum; the mid-Victorian Assembly Rooms, further up the street, now house an arts centre. The Radnorshire Arms is early 17th century. The town faces into England and has more of a Herefordshire look about it than many of its Border neighbours.

Pilleth 100

The church of St Mary, which stands isolated on the hillside above Pilleth Court, is approached from the fields by a wide flight of steps. Several medieval features remain, including the tower. The barn-like interior was not improved by a devastating fire in the last century. An isolated clump of wellingtonia trees above the church commemorates the Battle of Pilleth, where Owain Glyndwr defeated the forces of Henry IV in 1402: graphically described in the opening scene of Shakespeare's play (Part I).

Knighton 103

For the *route through Knighton*, climb up Broad Street, past the clock tower and continue on West Street to the former primary school 104, now a centre of Offa's Dyke activities (see page 126). The Path crosses the recreation ground beneath: note the coronation 'ER' planting in Kinsley Woods opposite 105. A sign points to a good stretch of Dyke just off the route which also has

Offa's Dyke at its full height, near Jenkin Allis.

the Stone which commemorates the opening of the Path by Lord Hunt in July 1971 before a mighty crowd. The Path goes through Pinner's Hole beneath the Dyke and descends to the picnic site by the River Teme. This is generally thought to be the Shropshire–Powys boundary, but *here* you are in England as the boundary marks an old course of the river!

'Tref y Clawdd', the Welsh name for Knighton, meaning 'town on the Dyke', makes clear its unique position as the only town where pronounced stretches of Offa's Dyke can be seen in the town itself. These are on the south side of the town crossing Frŷdd Road and then climbing up from the Cwm to follow the line of Offa's Road, and on the west side of the park north of West Street, overlooking the River Teme. The English name means 'town of the horsemen' (the original meaning of 'knight'), again suggesting its strategic significance in the defence of the Marches.

There are two castle sites, both now just mounds, one completely surrounded by buildings among the complicated network of small streets above the town centre; it can just be seen behind the fire station in Market Street. The other, probably earlier site, Bryn y Castell, is in the recreation ground behind the community centre in Bowling Green Lane. From the top there are splendid views up and down the Teme Valley and to the other castle mound.

Knighton nestling among the hills.

Knighton is a busy and prosperous market town. While there are few outstanding buildings, there are many interesting ones of different periods. One of the oldest is the medieval cruck-built Old House, hidden away behind the main frontage at the top of Broad Street, near the inevitable clock tower (almost indistinguishable from that at Hay: these must have come 'off the peg'!). From here the narrow High Street rises steeply to the Market Place, with mainly 17th century shops and other small buildings. This old part of town was built on the high ridge leading from and perhaps in the outer bailey of the castle. To the south it falls steeply to the Cwm, where small, haphazardly arranged cottages suggest a more informal settlement. St Edward's Church is on the north side of town: as with so many Border churches, only the tower is medieval, the rest is 1876–97.

The *Offa's Dyke Centre* **104** in West Street, in the southern corner of the Park containing a stretch of Offa's Dyke, is the former primary school. The local Tref y Clawdd Society rescued the building and it now houses a youth hostel, currently (1994) closed awaiting structural repairs, the Offa's Dyke Association Information Office, an exhibition about King Offa, the Dyke and the Border area generally, and a library on these topics. The Information Office serves the general visitor to Knighton as well as the specialist Dyke walker and stocks a range of maps, guides and souvenirs.

A number of *circular walks* from Knighton, exploring the Teme Valley and surrounding hill country, are well documented in a booklet produced by the Offa's Dyke Association. It can be obtained from the Knighton Information Office.

Border railways

Knighton is a suitable place to refer to the railways of the Border, since it has a station on the Heart of Wales Line from Shrewsbury to Llanelli and Swansea, which has remained open against all the odds. The line was built in sections by four different companies between 1857 and 1868, passing through magnificent but sparsely populated country. A survey we did as long ago as 1969 showed that for many people without cars in isolated settlements it is the only real link with 'civilisation'. Buses, on the steep and winding roads, take an unconscionable time for any but short journeys. Recent developments, through the active Heart of Wales Line Travellers' Association, have also demonstrated how a railway can encourage tourism. The Knighton station is now only a 'halt' but the elaborate 1861 Gothic-style building survives.

While this line survived the 'Beeching closures' of the 1960s, others serving the Border disappeared then or even earlier. Monmouth, once served by four lines, is now railwayless as are Hay-on-Wye, Kington, Oswestry and Llangollen – apart from a stretch of preserved line and steam trains and exhibits: a 'must' for the enthusiast. The other preserved line near the Path, this time narrow-gauge, is the delightful one from Welshpool to Llanfair Caereinion. Welshpool also has a British Rail line, which you cross at nearby Buttington. Other operational railways serving the Path are at Chepstow, Abergavenny, Chirk and Prestatyn.

The Welsh Border had networks of early horse-drawn tramways and of small industrial railway lines. These are mentioned in the text where remains are visible. This whole topic is of endless fascination to the railway enthusiast.

The centre of Knighton (Tref y Clawdd), the mid-point of the Path.

PART THREE

USEFUL
INFORMATION

This section includes much information that relates to both the southern and northern guides to Offa's Dyke Path, since readers are likely to find this helpful when planning to walk the Path.

Transport

Visitors from large towns will be disappointed with what is available, but must remember the sparse population of the area. Some years ago a member of a party we were leading asked why we needed to rush to catch a particular bus at the end of a walk: 'Can't we get the next one?' 'Same time next week' had to be the reply! Services have not improved since.

In general you can use public transport to get to and from many points on the Path, but services are usually too limited to be of much help for travel between the end of a day's walk and overnight accommodation elsewhere, except from Chepstow to Monmouth and Buttington to Llanymynech. In addition, services do come and go and the deregulation policies on buses have made services less predictable than before: even operators covering a particular area can change.

The Offa's Dyke Association's annual *Where to Stay* guide has a section on public transport which, though it does not give timetables, does provide accurate lists of operators and contact points as at the start of each year. Such lists in a book with the life of this volume would only mislead, but some relevant key information follows.

Rail
There are six relevant lines (the nearest point to the Path is in capitals). Phone (0345) 484950 for General Rail Enquiries.

Birmingham–Gloucester–CHEPSTOW–Cardiff (Wales and West)

Crewe–Shrewsbury–ABERGAVENNY (then catch a Hereford bus to PANDY)–Newport (Wales and West)

Shrewsbury–KNIGHTON–Llanelli–Swansea (Wales and West. The Heart of Wales Line Travellers' Association, Frankville, Broad Street, Llandovery, Dyfed, SA20 0AR, fights hard to promote this rural line and is worth your support.)

Shrewsbury–WELSHPOOL (over 2 miles/3 km)–Aberystwyth (Central Trains)

Wolverhampton–Shrewsbury–GOBOWEN–CHIRK (both over 2 miles/3 km)–Chester (Central Trains)

Chester–PRESTATYN–Bangor–Holyhead (a frequent service) (Northwestern Trains/Virgin Rail)

Long-distance coaches

These serve Chepstow, Monmouth, Abergavenny, Kington, Welshpool, Oswestry, Chirk, Llangollen and Prestatyn. Services are seldom more than one a day, though there are often extra services in summer, and advance booking is needed. Interchange points such as Birmingham and Cheltenham mean that most services are accessible from towns in England, with through booking facilities. Your guide is the *National Express Timetable*: most libraries have copies, as do local bus operators who usually also act as booking agents.

Local buses

There are two separate but linked networks: the commercial services considered by operators to be profitable, and supplementary services put out to tender by county councils to fill in the gaps. Companies can change, or withdraw, their own services at six weeks' notice. It is then up to the county council whether gaps thus created are filled. Subsidised services are reviewed annually. Thus, intending users must check the current position first with the Public Transport section of the appropriate county council (listed below), and possibly with the operators. No one operator has a monopoly on any part of the Path, though 'Red and White' is the major operator south of Monmouth as is 'Crosville' north of Welshpool.

County council Public Transport sections

Gloucestershire	—Gloucester (01452) 425609
Monmouthshire	—Newport (01633) 262914
Hereford & Worcester	—Worcester (01905) 766799 or Hereford (01432) 260948/260949
Shropshire	—(0345) 056785 (local call rates)
Powys	—Llandrindod Wells (01597) 826642
Flintshire	—Mold (01352) 704035

Twyn y Gaer and Sugar Loaf as seen from the southern slopes of Hatterrall H

Accommodation

For a wide range of accommodation you are restricted to the major towns and tourist centres. For the southern half, these are Chepstow (half a mile/0.8 km from the Path), Tintern (1 mile/1.6 km), Monmouth, Hay-on-Wye and Kington (on the Path), Presteigne (2½ miles/4 km) and Knighton (on the Path).

Several of the villages have an inn and a bed and breakfast establishment, but no greater choice. On or near the Path are St Briavels (1 mile/1.6 km), Redbrook, Llantilio Crossenny, Llangattock Lingoed, Pandy, Longtown (2 miles/3 km), Llanthony (2 miles) and Gladestry.

However, except for the Black Mountains stretch, these are supplemented by many farms which have, over the years since the Path opened, catered for the needs of walkers.

Any accommodation list is history even before it is printed. Most up-to-date is the Offa's Dyke Association's annual *Where to Stay* guide (see address on page 139), which lists many farms as well as the more usual hotels and guesthouses. It also has transport and other useful information.

Stilwell's *National Trail Companion* is an annual publication which lists accomodation for Offa's Dyke Path and other long-distance walks.

Other useful annual lists, covering a wider geographical area, are those from:

Ramblers' Association, 1/5 Wandsworth Road, London, SW8 2XX. They are of course the umbrella organisation for walkers' interests and problems. Their Yearbook is free to members and indicates bed and breakfast accommodation near all national trails.

Wales Tourist Board, Brunel House, Fitzalan Road, Cardiff, CF2 1UY. Heart of England Tourist Board, Larkhill Road, Worcester, WR5 2EZ. Between them, the two boards cover the Welsh and English sides of the Path.

Youth hostels

There are now (1994) only three relevant to the southern part of the Path (not equally spaced) at: St Briavels Castle (1½ miles/2.5 km), Monmouth (on route) and Capel-y-ffin (nearly 2½ miles/3.8 km). Chepstow has now closed and Knighton (on route and in the same building as the Offa's Dyke Centre) is currently (1994) closed pending structural repairs.

Further details, and membership of the YHA, from Trevelyan House, 8 St Stephen's Hill, St Albans, Herts, AL1 2DY.

Camping
A few large permanent sites are quoted in the Offa's Dyke Association *Where to Stay* list but most walkers' camping is done, fairly informally, by arrangement with farms passed on the walk. The Association also publishes a separate *Camping List* which covers those farms where, at the time of publication, camping is permitted: this list is updated regularly. Backpackers in particular are advised that they must not just camp anywhere: the permission of the farmer or owner is essential.

Caravan sites and holiday lettings
Most mobile caravanners will be members of the Camping and Caravanning Club of Great Britain and Ireland, 11 Grosvenor Place, London, SW1W 0EY, whose excellent directory gives information on sites available. The accommodation guides referred to above all include sections on caravans and holiday homes let for self-catering.

Cycling and horseriding

Offa's Dyke Path is a footpath with several hundred stiles. There are few sections of any length that are bridleways and thus suitable for horseriders or cyclists: those that exist have been marked on the maps. The longest sections are from Gladestry to Kington over Hergest Ridge (4½ miles/7 km), and the river route from Brockweir to Bigsweir (3 miles/5 km, but bridleway and Path diverge part way), and a stretch north from Dolley Green, north of Kington. There is much pony trekking in the Black Mountains but the Path here is not a bridleway.

Equipment

Compared with, say, the Pennine Way, Offa's Dyke is an 'easy' walk seldom far from town or village. Thus the need to carry enough equipment for emergencies to cover walking the whole route is reduced. Nevertheless the usual walker's rules of proper waterproofs, emergency warm clothing and rations, compass and whistle are sensible, especially over the moorland sections. Light walking boots are the all-purpose footwear: those who have a car or are doing day walks might like to have trainers, and also wellingtons, available to suit particular weather conditions.

Overall, travel as lightly loaded as safety allows as this will ease your way over the numerous stiles along the Path. For the backpacker there are shops *en route* where you can buy food and other provisions rather than carry all your needs from the start. Buying locally helps the rural economy and is one way of showing your appreciation of the countryside.

Facilities for walkers

It is impracticable to list every shop and other useful facility in the text, and you should refer to the maps where useful features are indicated (although, in some cases, things may have changed since the maps were prepared). These include public transport, inns, cafés, shops and post offices, phone boxes, public toilets, picnic sites and information centres. Some car parking is indicated but, for obvious reasons, not the sort of spot where one car can just be squeezed on to a verge. Concentration has been on the route itself but, where we could, we have also noted towns, villages and access points a little way off. Medical services, banks and also a range of shops are to be found only in the towns; many of these stay open quite late. Elsewhere there are only the village shops, but the range of goods in these should not be underestimated. Most inns now serve food.

Early closing days in the major centres are:

Tuesday   – Hay-on-Wye
Wednesday – Chepstow, Tintern, Kington, Knighton and Clun
Thursday   – Monmouth, Abergavenny, Presteigne, Welsh-
              pool, Oswestry, Chirk, Llangollen, Ruthin,
              Mold, Denbigh, St Asaph, Rhuddlan, Prestatyn
Saturday   – Montgomery

Visiting places of interest

The text of the book has tried to indicate the range of what is worth seeing a little off the route as well as on it. Towns, castles and abbeys are described in the features and circular walks, and the relevant tourist boards (referred to under 'Accommodation' above) have guide literature on the wider areas.

The principal ancient monuments are in the care of: (England) English Heritage, Fortress House, 43 Savile Row, London, W1X 2HE, and (Wales) Cadw (Welsh Historic Monuments), Brunel House, 2 Fitzalan Road, Cardiff, CF2 1UY, both of which publish annual lists of opening times and charges.

The National Trust, 36 Queen Anne's Gate, London, SW1H 9AS is responsible for the Kymin and Powis and Chirk Castles. Their handbook gives opening times and a wealth of other information about all their properties.

Offa's Dyke Association

The Offa's Dyke Association was set up in 1969 by the late Frank Noble, MBE, to campaign for the opening of the Path. It has continued ever since as a body linking walkers, conservationists and historians and those who live and work locally – and are affected by the tourism created by the Path. Nearly 30,000 callers and correspondents, mostly seeking information on walking the Path and on local amenities, are dealt with each year at its office in Knighton. A range of its own specialist guides, maps, accommodation lists and equipment is produced and kept up-to-date. The office is open daily from Easter to October and weekdays (at least) in winter.

Apart from this, the Association is active in Path maintenance and problems, and in conserving its natural and historical environment. It manages the Offa's Dyke Centre in Knighton (in the same building as the Youth Hostel, see page 136), which provides an Information Centre for the whole path and for the town, an exhibition on Offa and his Dyke, and headquarters for the Path Development staff. The Association is a membership body: its work is mainly dependent on its volunteers and on income from subscriptions and sales. It would welcome all Dyke-walkers to join its 1,000-strong band.

For a publication/sales list or membership form, write to Offa's Dyke Association (CC), West Street, Knighton, Powys, LD7 1EW. Please enclose a stamped, addressed envelope.

Other organisations

Many other organisations are concerned with aspects of the Welsh Marches, the Dyke and Path. The roles of the Ramblers' Association, the YHA and tourist boards have been mentioned under 'Accommodation', and of English Heritage, Cadw and the National Trust under 'Visiting places of interest'.

The Countryside Council for Wales and the Countryside Agency are responsible for National Trails (see page 22). Their addresses are Plas Penrhos, Ffordd Penrhos, Bangor, Gwynedd, LL57 2LQ and John Dower House, Crescent Place, Cheltenham, GL50 3RA respectively. Path maintenance is carried out for them by the local county councils, by the departments concerned with highways. The Trail Officer responsible for the Path is based at the Offa's Dyke Centre, West Street, Knighton, Powys LD7 1EN. (Telephone: 01547 528192; Fax: 01547 529242; email: oda@offasdyke.demon.co.uk).

The Brecon Beacons National Park, 7 Glamorgan Street, Brecon, Powys, LD3 7DP can provide information about the Black Mountains area through which Offa's Dyke Path runs.

The Clwyd-Powys Archaeological Trust, 7a Church Street, Welshpool, Powys, SY21 7DL and Manchester University Extra-Mural Department, The University, Manchester, M13 9PL have been the most active bodies in recent years in archaeological work on the Dyke.

Council for the Protection of Rural England (CPRE), Warwick House, 25 Buckingham Palace Road, London SW1W 0PP and CPRW, its Welsh counterpart, Ty Gwyn, 31 High Street, Welshpool, Powys, SY21 7JP work in the fields their titles suggest.

Most counties now have conservation or wildlife trusts. A full list can be obtained from the Royal Society for Nature Conservation, The Green, Witham Park, Waterside South, Lincoln, LN5 7JR. The Inland Waterways Association, 114 Regent's Park Road, London, NW1 8UG is the umbrella organisation for restoration of canals, such as the Montgomery. The Woodland Trust, Autumn Park, Dysart Road, Grantham, Lincs, NG31 6LL promotes, and owns, amenity woodland, such as that near Bigsweir (see page 38). The Royal Society for the Protection of Birds (RSPB), The Lodge, Sandy, Beds, SG19 2DL is what its title says.

Ordnance Survey, Romsey Road, Maybush, Southampton, SO9 4DH is the National Mapping Agency of Great Britain, publishing a wide range of maps for popular and professional use.

Bibliography

Choosing books for further reading is invidious: what follows is what we, over many years, have found useful and entertaining.

Path guides

Noble, Frank, *Offa's Dyke Path* (Offa's Dyke Association, 1981): by the man who did so much to bring Offa's Dyke Path into being.

Richards, Mark, *Through Welsh Border Country following Offa's Dyke Path* (Thornhill, 1976): a 'Wainwright'-style hand-drawn guide.

Wright, Christopher, *A Guide to Offa's Dyke Path* (Constable, 1986, 2nd edition): very detailed on towns and monuments on or near the Path.

Welsh Border generally

Fraser, Maxwell, *Welsh Border Country* (Batsford, 1972).

Millward, R. and Robinson, A., *The Welsh Border* (Eyre Methuen, 1978).

Stanford, S. C., *Archaeology of the Welsh Marches* (revised edition, 1991, published by author).

Dyke archaeology

Fox, Sir Cyril, *Offa's Dyke* (British Academy, 1955): a detailed account of the key 1920s/30s survey.

Hill, David, articles in *Mediaeval Archaeology* on the recent work by Manchester University Extra-Mural Department.

Noble, Frank, edited by Gelling, M., *Offa's Dyke Reviewed* (BAR British Series 114, 1983): the most thorough modern analysis of the Dyke.

Stenton, Sir Frank, *Anglo Saxon England* (Oxford University Press, 1943, 3rd edition 1971) is the best comprehensive guide to the history of the period.

Trueman, A. E., *Geology and Scenery in England and Wales* (Penguin, 1949) is the best and simplest exponent on this topic.

Buildings

The Penguin *Buildings of England and Wales* series, edited and mostly written by Sir Nikolaus Pevsner, is unbeatable. Relevant volumes are those on Gloucestershire: the Vale and Forest of Dean, Herefordshire, Shropshire, Clwyd and Powys. There is no Gwent volume yet: we found Bobby Freeman's *Gwent* (Robin Clark, 1980) useful. For specific properties in their care the guides of Cadw, English Heritage and the National Trust are essential.

Alternative relevant paths

'Castles' Alternative': Monmouth to Hay, and 'Knighton Circuits' are devised by Offa's Dyke Association, which has booklets on each.

Glyndwr's Way: Knighton to Machynlleth and back to Welshpool, is covered by a set of leaflets from Powys County Council and Richard Sale, *Owain Glyndwr's Way* (new edition, Constable, 1992). This route is currently (1994) being considered for upgrading to National Trail status.

Wye Valley Walk: Chepstow to Ross, Hereford, Hay-on-Wye, Builth Wells and Rhyader. Gwent, Powys, and Hereford and

Worcestershire County Councils have guides for their sections of this route.

'Period' books

Borrow, George, *Wild Wales* (Everyman Library): an 1861 travel book.

Hogg, Garry, *And Far Away* (Dent, 1946): the first book about walking the Dyke, well before the existence of Offa's Dyke Path.

Kilvert's Diary, edited by Plomer, W. (Jonathan Cape, 1964; Penguin, reissued 1984): this one-volume selection is a good sample of the now-famous evocative mid-Victorian description of life in the Clyro/Hay area.

Mabinogion, The (Everyman Library): the source book for Welsh legends.

Watkins, Alfred, *The Old Straight Track* (Methuen, 1925, reprinted Abacus, 1974): an exposition of one theory about many of our ancience monuments.

Fiction

Chatwin, Bruce, *On the Black Hill* (Jonathan Cape, 1982; Picador, 1983): now a film and play too.

Williams, Raymond, *Border Country* (Chatto & Windus, 1960): life between the Wars in the East Wales valleys.

The historical novels of Edith Pargeter, such as *The Heaven Tree*, and *The Secret of Grey Walls* and other children's stories by Malcolm Saville, are relevant and evocative of the Welsh Borders, as is the verse of A. E. Housman in *A Shropshire Lad*.

Other

Davies, Dewi, *Welsh Place Names and Their Meaning* (Cambrian Press).

Rees, W., *A Historical Atlas of Wales* (Faber & Faber, 1951).

There are many excellent guides and histories to particular towns and areas, and volumes on canal and railway history, but space does not allow more than a passing reference to these topics.

Ordnance Survey Maps covering the Offa's Dyke Path
(listed from north to south)
Landranger Maps (1:50 000): 116, 117, 126, 137, 148, 161, 162.
1:25 000 scale maps: Pathfinder 737 (SJ08/18), Pathfinder 755 (SJ07/17), Pathfinder 772 (SJ06/16), Pathfinder 788 (SJ05/15), Explorer 256 (Wrexham & Llangollen), Pathfinder 827 (SJ23/33), Pathfinder 847 (SJ22/32), Pathfinder 868 (SJ21/31), Explorer 216 (Welshpool & Montgomery), Explorer 201 (Knighton & Presteigne), Outdoor Leisure 13 (Brecon Beacons–Eastern area), Outdoor Leisure 14 (Wye Valley & Forest of Dean)
Motoring Maps: Reach Offa's Dyke Path using Travelmaster 7 (Wales & West Midlands)

Glossary of Welsh place names

Welsh place names are usually descriptions, some of them quite poetic. But the emphasis is on description. Many places begin with the word *aber*, meaning the mouth of a river. Aberystwyth, the mouth of Ystwyth River; Abertawe (the Welsh name for Swansea), the mouth of the Tawe River. Another class of place name begins with the word *llan*, a church or parish. Llanfair, the church of (St) Mary; Llanfihangel, the church of (St) Michael.

Plurals in Welsh are usually formed by adding the letters AU to the end of a word. An example is *dol* (a meadow); *dolau* (meadows).

A small Welsh-English pocket dictionary (see page 142) would be a useful companion in any walker's rucksack. But for the impecunious here is a small glossary of common words and their meanings:

Bach, fach, small	*Dyffryn,* valley
Bryn, hill	*Llyn,* lake
Bwlch, pass	*Llys,* hall or palace
Caer, gaer, fort	*Maen,* stone
Cefn, ridge	*Mawr, fawr,* big
Clawdd, dyke	*Melin,* mill
Coed, wood	*Nant,* stream
Du, black	*Pont,* bridge
Dwr, water	*Ty,* house